Camp Creations
Crafts for kids

Camp Bugaboo

Rugged Cross

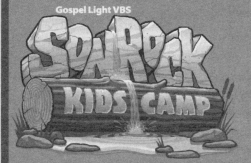

REPRODUCIBLE

- Fun at Church, Home or School
- 45 Fun Craft Projects for all ages

Includes
CD-ROM

This year's summer camp theme gives each activity center the opportunity to bring to life a different fun camp location. The Craft Center takes place in the Craft Cabin and features crafts that will help kids remember their fun-filled visit to SonRock Kids Camp. Kids will get to let their creativity flow as they create crafts that will emphasize Bible stories, Bible verses, the Daily Truths and more! As leaders of this center, give yourself a fun camp name like Artsy Annie or Crafty Kate. Dress in camp clothes. Make the theme come alive for your VBS students! You'll have as much fun as the kids—maybe more!

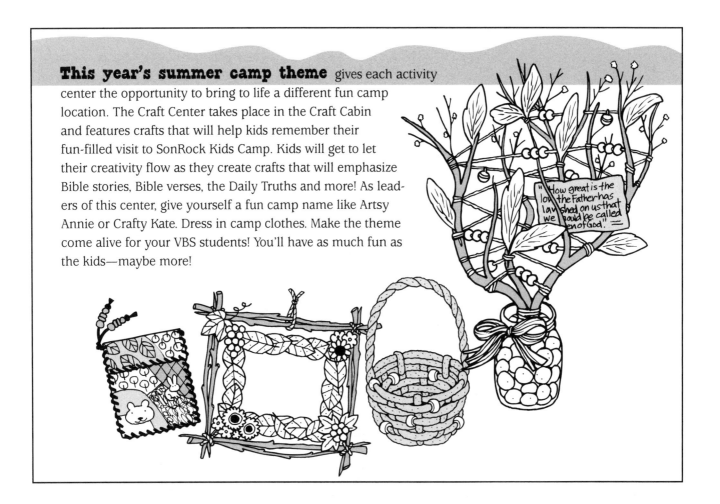

Guidelines for Photocopying Reproducible Pages

Permission to make photocopies of or to reproduce by any other mechanical or electronic means in whole or in part any designated* page, illustration or activity in this book is granted only to the original purchaser and is intended for noncommercial use within a church or other Christian organization. None of the material in this book, not even those pages with permission to photocopy, may be reproduced for any commercial promotion, advertising or sale of a product or service or to share with any other persons, churches or organizations. Sharing of the material in this book with other churches or organizations not owned or controlled by the original purchaser is also prohibited. All rights reserved.

*Do not make any copies from this book unless you adhere strictly to the guidelines found on this page. Pages with the following notation can be legally reproduced:

Gospel Light Vacation Bible School

Senior Managing Editor, Sheryl Haystead
Associate Editor, Janis Halverson
Contributing Writers, Cindy Ethier, Kim Fiano, Karen McGraw
Contributing Editors, Sheila Barnish, Jane Eilert, Susan Hill, Leanna Sheppard
Art Directors, Lori Hamilton, Lenndy Pollard, Jessica Morrison
Senior Designer, Carolyn Thomas

Founder, Dr. Henrietta Mears
Publisher, William T. Greig
Senior Consulting Publisher, Dr. Elmer L. Towns
Senior Consulting Editor, Wesley Haystead, M.S.Ed.
Senior Editor, Theology and Biblical Content, Dr. Gary S. Greig

Contents

Introduction

Summer Camp Fun!

Going to summer camp means exploring nature, building friendships, learning new skills and creating exciting memories with family and friends. Children of all ages love summer camp! The breathtaking atmosphere of SonRock Kids Camp inspired the crafts found in this resource book. We hope that you and your campers enjoy many fun-filled hours creating projects from *Camp Creations Crafts for Kids*.

Personalize It!

Feel free to alter the craft materials and instructions in this book to suit your children's needs. Consider what materials you have on hand, what materials are available in your area and what materials you can afford to purchase. In some cases, you may be able to substitute materials you already have for the suggested craft supplies.

In addition, don't feel confined to the crafts in a particular age-level section. You may want to adapt a craft for younger or older children by using the simplification or enrichment ideas where provided.

Three Keys to Success

How can you make craft time successful and fun for your children? First, encourage creativity in each child! Remember, the process of creating is more important than the final product. Provide a variety of materials with which children may work. Allow children to make choices on their own. Don't insist that children "stay inside the lines."

Second, choose projects that are appropriate for the skill level of your children. Children can become discouraged when a project is too difficult for them. Finding the right projects for your children will increase the likelihood that they will be successful and satisfied with their finished products.

Finally, show an interest in the unique way each child approaches a project. Affirm the choices he or she has made. Treat each child's final product as a masterpiece!

The comments you give a child today can affect the way he or she views art in the future, so be positive! Being creative is part of being made in the image of God, the ultimate creator!

Craft Symbols

Many of the craft projects in *Camp Creations Crafts for Kids* are appropriate for more than one age level. Next to the title of certain projects, you'll find the symbol shown below. This symbol tells which projects are suitable or adaptable for all elementary-age children—first through sixth grades. As you select projects, consider the particular children you are working with. Feel free to use your own ideas to make projects simpler or more challenging, depending on the needs of your children.

In addition, some craft projects in this book require less preparation than others. The symbol shown below tells which projects require minimal preparation.

suitable for all ages   minimal preparation

Crafts with a Message

Many projects in *Camp Creations Crafts for Kids* can easily become crafts with a message. Have children create slogans or add the Daily Truths as part of their projects; or provide photocopies of an appropriate thought or Bible verse for children to attach to their crafts. Below are some examples of ways to use messages to enhance the craft projects in this book.

Conversation

Each craft in this book includes a Conversation section designed to help you enhance craft times with thought-provoking conversation that is age appropriate. The Conversation section for a project may relate to prayer, a Scripture verse or a Bible story. Often Conversation sections will include interesting facts. If your craft program includes large groups of children, share these Conversation suggestions with each helper, who can use them with individuals or small groups.

Be Prepared

If you are planning to use crafts with a child at home, here are some helpful tips:

- Focus on crafts designed for your child's age, but don't ignore projects for older or younger ages. Elementary-age children enjoy many of the projects geared for preschool and kindergarten children. And younger children are always interested in doing "big kid" things. Just plan on working along with your child, helping with tasks he or she can't handle alone.

- Start with projects that call for materials you have around the house. Make a list of items you do not have, and plan to gather them in one expedition.

- If certain materials seem too difficult to obtain, a little thought can usually lead to appropriate substitutions. Often your creative twist ends up being an improvement over the original plan.

If you are planning to lead a group of children in doing craft projects, keep these hints in mind:

- Choose projects that allow children to work with a variety of materials.

- Make your project selections far enough in advance to allow time to gather all needed supplies.

- Make a sample of each project to be sure the directions are fully understood and potential problems can be avoided. **You may want to adapt some projects by simplifying procedures or varying the materials.**

- Items can often be acquired as donations from people or businesses if you plan ahead and make your needs known. Many churches distribute lists of needed materials to their congregations. Some items can be brought by the children themselves.

- In making your supply list, distinguish between items that each individual child will need and those that will be shared among a group.

- Keep in mind that some materials may be shared among more than one age level. To avoid frustration, coordinate with other groups that might be using the same supplies you need so that children can complete their craft projects. Basic supplies that are used in many projects, such as glue, scissors, markers, etc., should be available in every craft room.

Helpful Hints

Using Glue with Young Children

Because preschoolers have difficulty using glue bottles effectively, you may want to try one of the following procedures. Purchase glue in large containers (up to one gallon size).

a. Pour small amounts of glue into several margarine tubs.

b. Dilute glue by mixing a little water into each container.

c. Children use paintbrushes to spread glue on their projects.

d. When project is completed, place lids on margarine tubs to save glue for future projects.

OR

a. Pour small amounts of glue into several margarine tubs.

b. Give each child a cotton swab.

c. Children dip cotton swabs into the glue and rub glue on projects.

d. When project is completed, place lids on margarine tubs to save glue for future projects.

Cutting with Scissors

When cutting with scissors is required for crafts, remember that some children in your class may be left-handed. It is very difficult for a left-handed person to cut with right-handed scissors. Have available two or three pairs of left-handed scissors. These can be obtained from a school-supply center.

If your craft involves cutting fabric, felt or ribbon, have available several pairs of fabric scissors for older children.

Using Acrylic Paints

Acrylic paints are required for several projects. Our suggestions:

- Provide smocks or old shirts for your children to wear, as acrylics may stain clothes.

- Acrylics can be expensive for a large group of children. To make paint go further, dilute it with a small amount of water. Or use house paints thinned with water.

- Fill shallow containers with soapy water. Clean paintbrushes before switching colors and immediately after finishing project.

Leading a Child to Christ

One of the greatest privileges of serving in VBS is helping children become members of God's family. Pray for the children you teach and ask God to prepare them to understand and receive the good news about Jesus. Ask God to give you the sensitivity and wisdom you need to communicate effectively and to be aware of opportunities that occur naturally.

Because children are easily influenced to follow the group, be cautious about asking for group decisions. Offer opportunities to talk and pray individually with any child who expresses interest in becoming a member of God's family—but without pressure. A good way to guard against coercing a child to respond is to simply ask, "Would you like to hear more about this now or at another time?"

When talking about salvation with children, use words and phrases they understand; never assume they understand a concept just because they can repeat certain words. Avoid symbolic terms ("born again," "ask Jesus to come into your heart," "open your heart," etc.) that will confuse these literal-minded thinkers. (You may also use the evangelism booklet *God Loves You!* available from Gospel Light.)

1. God wants you to become His child. Why do you think He wants you in His family? (See 1 John 3:1.)
2. You and I and every person in the world has done wrong things. The Bible word for doing wrong is "sin." What do you think should happen to us when we sin? (See Romans 6:23.)
3. God loves you so much that He sent His Son to die on the cross to take the punishment for your sin. Because Jesus never sinned, He is the only One who can take the punishment for your sin. On the third day after Jesus died, God brought Him back to life. (See 1 Corinthians 15:3-4; 1 John 4:14.)
4. Are you sorry for your sin? Tell God that you are. Do you believe Jesus died for your sin and then rose again? Tell Him that, too. If you tell God you are sorry for your sin and believe that Jesus died to take your sin away, God forgives you. (See 1 John 1:9.)
5. The Bible says that when you believe that Jesus is God's Son and that He is alive today, you receive God's gift of eternal life. This gift makes you a child of God. This means God is with you now and forever. (See John 1:12; 3:16.)

There is great value in encouraging a child to think and pray about what you have said before responding. Encourage the child who makes a decision to become a Christian to tell his or her parents. Give your pastor and the child's Sunday School teacher(s) his or her name. A child's initial response to Jesus is just the beginning of a lifelong process of growing in the faith, so children who make decisions need to be followed up to help them grow. The discipling booklet *Growing as God's Child* (available from Gospel Light) is an effective tool to use.

Age-Level Characteristics

Ages 3 to 6

Preschool and kindergarten crafts have been planned for children who are three to six years old with a ratio of one teacher for every 4 to 6 children. Each craft provides enough flexibility so that young children can work successfully. Effectively instructing children of varying ages requires a teacher to recognize and accept wide individual differences in skills, abilities and interests. Regardless of the level at which a child works, a teacher can use the child's interest in the activity to guide his or her thinking toward understanding a Bible truth.

THREES and FOURS are just beginning to use art supplies and often find the finished product of little interest. Encourage them to try new things, but don't expect beauty or design.

KINDERGARTNERS enjoy exploring the use of art materials but may find the process tedious after a short while. To sustain their interest, offer encouragement and assistance as needed.

Grades 1 and 2

The term "perpetual motion" may be used to describe children this age. Small-muscle coordination is still developing and improving. Girls are ahead of boys at this stage of development.

Children are concerned with pleasing their leaders. Each child is also struggling to become socially acceptable to the peer group. The Golden Rule is a tough concept at this age. Being first and winning are very important. Taking turns is hard, but this skill improves by the end of the second grade. A child's social process moves gradually from *I* to *you* and *we*.

Provide opportunities for children to practice taking turns. Help each child accept the opinions and wishes of others and consider the welfare of the group as well as his or her own welfare. Call attention to times when the group cooperated successfully.

Children are experiencing new and frequently intense feelings as they grow in independence. Sometimes the child finds it hard to control his or her behavior. There is still a deep need for approval from adults and a growing need for approval by peers.

Seek opportunities to help each child in your group KNOW and FEEL you love him or her. Show genuine interest in each child and his or her activities and accomplishments. Learn children's names and use them frequently in positive ways.

Grades 3 and 4

Children at this level have good large- and small-muscle coordination. The girls are generally ahead of the boys. Children can work diligently for longer periods but can become impatient with delays or their own imperfect abilities.

Children's desire for status within the peer group becomes more intense. Most children remain shy with strangers and exhibit strong preferences for being with a few close friends. Some children still lack essential social skills needed to make and retain friendships.

Look for the child who needs a friend. Move near that child and include him or her in what you are doing.

This is the age of teasing, nicknames, criticism and increased verbal skills to vent anger. By eight years of age, children have developed a sense of fair play and a value system of right and wrong. At nine years of age, children are searching for identity beyond membership in the family unit.

You have a great opportunity to be a Christian example at a time when children are eagerly searching for models! Encourage children's creativity and boost their self-concept. Let children know by your words and by your actions that "love is spoken here" and that you will not let others hurt them or let them hurt others.

Grades 5 and 6

Children have mastered most basic physical skills, are active and curious, and seek a variety of new experiences. Rapid growth can cause some 11-year-olds to tire easily. Oftentimes in coed groups, boys tend to be less aggressive and girls tend to be friendlier. The mixture seems to bring out the best in both genders.

Friendships and activities with their peers flourish. Children draw together and away from adults in the desire for independence. The child wants to be a part of a same-gender group and usually does not want to stand alone in competition.

Children are usually cooperative, easygoing, content, friendly and agreeable. Be aware that often 11-year-old children are experiencing unsteady emotions and can quickly shift from one mood to another.

Be patient with changes of feelings. Give many opportunities to make choices with only a few necessary limits. Take time to listen as students share their experiences and problems with you.

Children of this age are verbal! Making ethical decisions becomes a challenging task. They are able to express ideas and feelings in a creative way. By 11 years old, children have begun to be able to reason abstractly. They begin to think of themselves as grown-up and at the same time question adult concepts. Hero worship is strong.

Include lots of opportunities for talking, questioning and discussing in a safe, accepting environment. Ask children for their ideas of how things could be done better.

If you'll be leading crafts at SonRock Kids Camp Vacation Bible School, *Camp Creation Crafts for Kids* contains more than enough crafts for each age level. For additional hints about leading a group of children in craft projects, see "Be Prepared" on page 5.

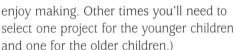

The projects in this book can be done in individual classrooms or in a Craft Center. Here's how a Craft Center works:

- Select projects that will appeal to several age levels. (Sometimes you'll find one project that all children will enjoy making. Other times you'll need to select one project for the younger children and one for the older children.)

- Recruit adults and/or youths to prepare for and run the Craft Center.

- Decorate your center with samples of crafts your kids will be making.

- As classes visit the Craft Center, lead them in making projects, tailoring instructions and conversation to the children's age level.

The Craft Coordinator— A Very Important Person

As Craft Coordinator, you play a key role in determining the quality of your craft program. Here are four crucial steps in achieving success at your task:

1. Plan ahead. Familiarize yourself with each day's craft project and plan any necessary changes.

2. Be well-organized (see "SonRock Kids Camp Countdown Schedule").

3. Secure your supplies in advance. Prepare a bulletin notice listing items you need donated from members of your congregation. Also, people are often happy to help if you personally ask them to donate or purchase specific items.

4. Communicate with everyone involved. People who do not know what to do may not ask for help.

SonRock Kids Camp Countdown Schedule

16 weeks before:

1. List all staff needs. (Determine if crafts will be led by regular teachers or by special craft leaders and if students from the Youth Department will serve as craft helpers.)

2. Meet with the VBS Director to compile a list of prospective staff.

3. Begin personal contacts to recruit needed staff.

12 weeks before:

1. Select projects from this book and list needed supplies.

2. Determine which items are already on hand and which need to be secured.

8 weeks before:

1. Distribute a bulletin notice listing needed supplies.

2. Begin organizing supplies as they are acquired. Separate inventories for each age group are often helpful, especially in large programs.

6 weeks before:

1. Review staffing needs with the VBS Director and plan involvement in training session.

2. Assign leaders to make a sample of each craft project that they will teach to children.

3. Distribute second notice regarding supplies.

Tip: Plan VBS craft preparation days. Have one or two during the day and at least one in the evening so that more volunteers can participate and be a part of VBS.

---

4 weeks before:

1. Participate in training session, showing samples of at least the first-day craft projects.

2. Distribute third notice regarding supplies.

3. Make any needed personal contacts to gather required supplies.

2 weeks before:

1. Purchase any supplies still needed. Adjust supplies as needed.

During VBS:

1. Make sure needed supplies are available for staff.

2. Secure additional supplies as needed.

Course Description

High above the cluttered schedules and ringing cell phones of ordinary life is SonRock Kids Camp—an outdoor adventure camp like no other! As SonRock campers, your students will learn how their lives can be transformed by God's great love for them: *How great is the love the Father has lavished on us, that we should be called children of God!* (1 John 3:1).

Nothing challenges a person to examine his or her identity quite like an adventure in God's great outdoors. And with easy-to-make decorations, your church facility can be transformed into an adventure site: A pristine forest to explore. Fascinating animals to observe. Opportunities to learn new skills and reach new heights as campers overcome obstacles they once may have thought impossible. But crisp mountain air and crystal clear streams of sweet water are only the beginning of what SonRock Kids Camp has to offer. Campers will build bonds of friendship with each other and with caring counselors as they discover that their true identities are not formed by where they go, what they can do or what others think. Like the apostle Peter, they'll explore who they are in Jesus Christ—the most important relationship of all. Because of His love for us, He is the rock upon which we can build our lives!

- As they watch Jesus call Peter away from his fishing nets, they'll discover what it means to be **Accepted by Jesus**.
- Later, when Jesus invites Peter to step out of the safety of a boat and onto a churning sea, they'll discover what it means to be **Protected by Jesus**.
- As they witness Peter's confession of Jesus as the Messiah, they'll learn how to be **Saved by Jesus**.
- From Peter's shocking denial and Jesus' redemptive forgiveness, they'll know that no sin is too large to be **Forgiven by Jesus**.
- Finally, as they discover how Peter's faith in Jesus made a lame man walk, they'll know the power of **Living for Jesus**.

This summer, send your kids to SonRock Kids Camp VBS—a mountaintop experience they'll never forget!

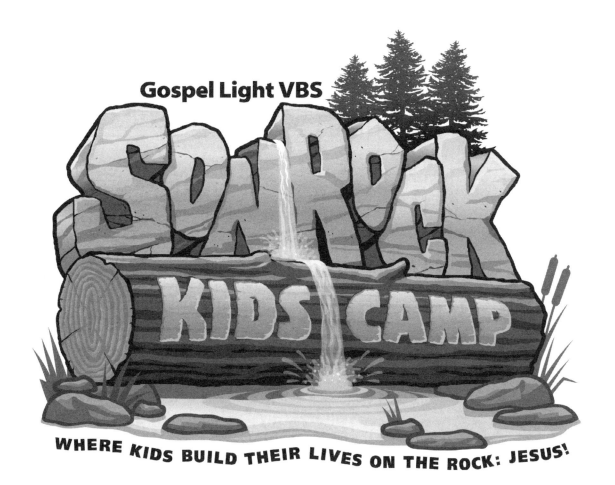

Gospel Light VBS

WHERE KIDS BUILD THEIR LIVES ON THE ROCK: JESUS!

Decorating Your Craft Center

SonRock Craft Cabin

Turn your Craft Center into the SonRock Craft Cabin!

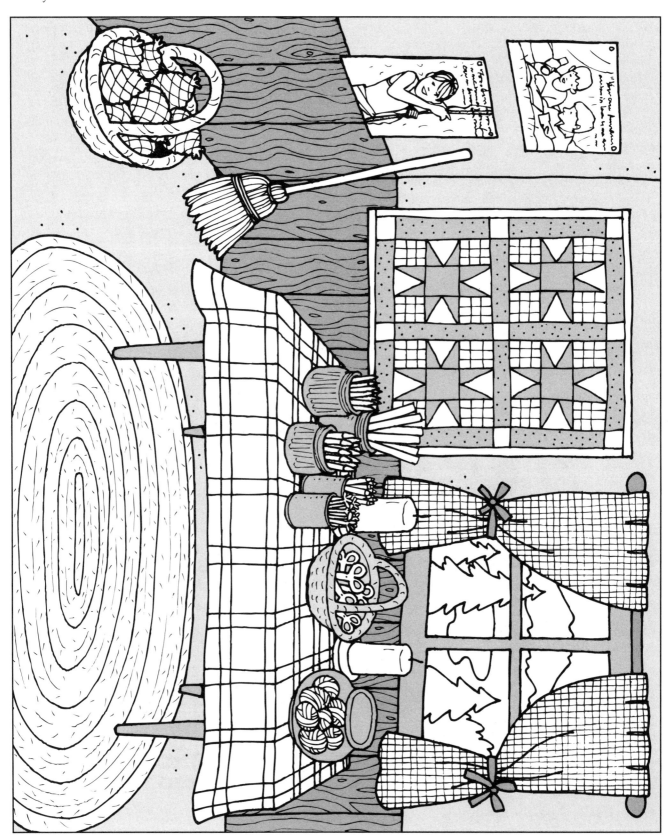

Course Overview and Suggested Crafts

Below is an overview of SonRock Kids Camp VBS with suggested projects for each age level. Each craft has been selected to reinforce the Bible story, lesson focus or memory verse of the day. All projects are fully described in this book.

Course Overview
Bible Theme: 1 John 3:1

Daily Truth	Bible Story	Who Am I?	Bible Memory Verse	Suggested Crafts
1 Accepted by Jesus	Catch of the Day: Jesus Chooses Peter Matthew 4:18-20; Luke 5:1-11; John 1:40-42	I am loved and accepted by Jesus.	**Early Childhood** "God loves us and calls us His children." (See 1 John 3:1.) **Elementary** "How great is the love the Father has lavished on us, that we should be called children of God!" 1 John 3:1	**Early Childhood** Fishing Poles **Primary** Rockin' Pendant **Middler** Nature Journal **Preteen** Nature Journal
2 Protected by Jesus	Wet and Wild Walk: Jesus Walks on Water Matthew 14:13-36	I am helped and protected by Jesus.	**Early Childhood** "God says, 'Do not fear; I will help you.'" (See Isaiah 41:13.) **Elementary** "I am the LORD, your God, who takes hold of your right hand and says to you, Do not fear; I will help you." Isaiah 41:13	**Early Childhood** Peter At Sea **Primary** Walking on Water Window **Middler** Nature Pouch **Preteen** Backpack It Up
3 Saved by Jesus	Tell It Like It Is: Peter's Confession of Christ Matthew 16:13-17; Matthew 26—28	I am given salvation and eternal life by Jesus, God's Son.	**Early Childhood** "Believe in Jesus and that He is alive." (See Romans 10:9.) **Elementary** "If you confess with your mouth, 'Jesus is Lord,' and believe in your heart that God raised him from the dead, you will be saved." Romans 10:9	**Early Childhood** Cross Necklace **Primary** Rugged Cross **Middler** Wire Wraps **Preteen** Nature Words
4 Forgiven by Jesus	A Rooster Crows: Peter Denies Jesus Matthew 26:31-35, 69-75; Luke 22:54-62; John 21:1-17	Even when I sin, Jesus forgives me and gives me a fresh start.	**Early Childhood** "You are forgiving and good, O Lord. You always love me." (See Psalm 86:5.) **Elementary** "You are forgiving and good, O Lord, abounding in love to all who call to you." Psalm 86:5	**Early Childhood** SonRock Backpack **Primary** Camp Bugaboo Cabin **Middler** Fresh Start Rainbow **Preteen** Flowering Tiles
5 Living for Jesus	Lame Man Leaping: Peter Helps a Lame Man Acts 3	I can live for Jesus and do the good things He has planned for me to do.	**Early Childhood** "God made us to do good things." (See Ephesians 2:10.) **Elementary** "For we are God's workmanship, created in Christ Jesus to do good works, which God prepared in advance for us to do." Ephesians 2:10	**Early Childhood** Camp Cabin Bank **Primary** Living for Jesus Calendar **Middler** Natural Frames **Preteen** Nature Object Candle

Catch of the Day:
Jesus Chooses Peter

Scripture

Matthew 4:18-20; Luke 5:1-11; John 1:40-42

Bible Memory Verse

How great is the love the Father has lavished on us, that we should be called children of God! 1 John 3:1

Who Am I?

I am loved and accepted by Jesus.

Bible Aims for Each Student

During this session, I may

1. TELL that Peter discovered that Jesus loved and accepted him when Jesus chose him to be His disciple;

2. DISCUSS times kids might not feel loved or accepted;

3. THANK Jesus for loving and accepting me, even when others don't;

4. CHOOSE to receive God's forgiveness and to become a member of God's family, as the Holy Spirit leads.

Bible Story Recap

When Simon the fisherman's brother Andrew introduced him to Jesus, Jesus promptly changed Simon's name to Peter. Later, Jesus explained He gave Peter this new name because he was going to become a solid, strong leader of the people who followed Jesus.

Then one day, Jesus asked Peter to take his boat out on the water, and throw his nets out to catch fish. Even though Peter had been fishing all night long and hadn't caught a thing, he did as Jesus asked. To his amazement, his fishing nets were so full of fish, they had to ask friends to help them pull the nets into the boats.

Jesus then asked Peter and his brother Andrew to follow him and become fishers of men. They happily left everything to follow Jesus.

Teacher's Devotional

Peter was an ordinary man with an ordinary career until Jesus came into his life. Jesus called Peter to follow Him and Peter responded. Did Peter know what he would be giving up or what he would be gaining by following Jesus?

As we look into Peter's life and experiences with Jesus, we will discover that ordinary Peter saw and did extraordinary things because of his willingness to follow Jesus. Peter experienced unconditional love and acceptance from Jesus. You made a decision to follow Jesus and lead campers at SonRock Kids Camp this week. You may feel ordinary and unsure of yourself, like Peter. Rest assured you are loved and accepted by Jesus! He has called you to serve Him and do extraordinary things by loving and leading the campers in your care. He will equip you to do all that is required of you.

As you prepare to meet your campers this week, ask the Lord to help you greet them warmly and be an extension of the unconditional love and acceptance Jesus has shown you.

Wet and Wild Walk: Jesus Walks on Water

Scripture

Matthew 14:13-36

Bible Memory Verse

I am the LORD, your God, who takes hold of your right hand and says to you, Do not fear; I will help you. Isaiah 41:13

Who Am I?

I am helped and protected by Jesus.

Bible Aims for Each Student

During this session, I may

1. REPORT that Jesus displayed His power and protected Peter when Peter was in danger;

2. IDENTIFY situations in which I can rely on Jesus' power and protection;

3. ASK Jesus' help to trust in His protection in every situation;

4. CHOOSE to receive God's forgiveness and to become a member of God's family, as the Holy Spirit leads.

Bible Story Recap

On the same day that Jesus fed 5,000 people with two fish and five small loaves of bread, He asked the disciples to leave Him alone to pray. The disciples left, sailing off over the Sea of Galilee.

Then a huge storm arose, rocking the small boat and frightening the disciples. All night long they battled the storm. Then in the early morning hours, they saw a figure on the water. "It's a ghost!" someone cried out.

But Peter heard a voice, "Have courage! It is I! Don't be afraid." Peter knew that voice! It was Jesus out there on the water. Peter got out of the boat and walked toward Jesus. But he looked down at the waves, grew afraid and started to sink. Jesus pulled Peter from the water, protecting him from the dangerous waves.

Teacher's Devotional

In today's story Peter took a great step of faith and actually walked on water! But then he lost sight of Jesus and began to sink. When he cried out to Jesus, Jesus was right there with His hand outstretched, protecting Peter from the surrounding danger.

Have you ever stepped out in faith and confidence only to find yourself frozen by fear? How did Jesus help you overcome your fear? Following Jesus does not guarantee peaceful waters. There will be raging storms and many trials in this world. Remember to be encouraged and have hope, for Jesus has overcome the fears of this world (see John 16:33).

The campers you encounter this week may be experiencing their own storms, some even raised by being at SonRock Kids Camp. Trying a new activity may cause anxiety in a child. Interacting with other children may be worrisome. You can help calm these kinds of storms by giving the child the choice to watch for a while and then join in when he or she feels ready.

Thank God for each of the campers in your care. Ask Him to show you ways to point them to Jesus' protection and help.

Tell It Like It Is: Peter's Confession of Christ

Saved by Jesus — 3

Scripture

Matthew 16:13-17; Matthew 26—28

Bible Memory Verse

If you confess with your mouth, "Jesus is Lord," and believe in your heart that God raised him from the dead, your will be saved. Romans 10:9

Who Am I?

I am given salvation and eternal life by Jesus, God's Son.

Bible Aims for Each Student

During this session, I may

1. TELL about the time Peter confessed that Jesus is the Savior;

2. DISCUSS what "salvation" and "eternal life" mean in my life;

3. THANK Jesus for His gifts of salvation and eternal life;

4. CHOOSE to receive God's forgiveness and to become a member of God's family, as the Holy Spirit leads.

Bible Story Recap

One day Jesus asked the disciples who people said He was. The disciples said people thought He was John the Baptist, Jeremiah, Elijah or one of the other prophets.

Then Jesus asked, "Who do YOU say that I am?" Peter must have thought about all the amazing things he'd seen Jesus do, and all the wonderful things Jesus had taught him about God. Then the Holy Spirit helped Peter understand exactly who Jesus is.

Peter said, "You are the Savior God promised to send." But not everyone believed Jesus was the Savior. Some people were angry with Jesus. They managed to get Jesus arrested and killed, even though Jesus had done nothing wrong. But Jesus didn't stay dead! Jesus rose from the tomb and is alive today! His death and resurrection prove He was the Savior.

Teacher's Devotional

Today SonRock campers will explore what it means to be saved. As a Jewish man, Peter had been taught about God's promised Savior. The realization that Jesus was that very Savior came to Peter through spending time with Jesus and by revelation of the Holy Spirit.

Just like Peter, each one of us has to decide who we believe Jesus is. Believing Jesus is the Christ causes a radical change in our lives. Our sins are forgiven and we are assured eternal life. Even more, proclaiming Jesus as Savior and Lord also gives us the incredible opportunity to fulfill the purpose for which we were created: to know Christ and to make Him known.

The idea of needing to be "saved" may be foreign to your campers. Read carefully the child-level explanations provided in this lesson. Pray for opportunities to help them understand the need to accept God's amazing gifts of salvation and eternal life. Think about the perfection of Jesus and the immeasurable love He displayed when He willingly paid the price for your sin and the sins of your campers. Ask Him to help you love each camper the way He does.

A Rooster Crows: Peter Denies Jesus

Scripture

Matthew 26:31-35, 69-75; Luke 22:54-62; John 21:1-17

Bible Memory Verse

You are forgiving and good, O Lord, abounding in love to all who call to you. Psalm 86:5

Who Am I?

Even when I sin, Jesus forgives me and gives me a fresh start.

Bible Aims for Each Student

During this session, I may

1. DISCOVER that even though Peter denied Jesus, he was forgiven by Jesus;

2. LIST and DISCUSS steps to forgiveness;

3. ASK Jesus for forgiveness and a fresh start;

4. CHOOSE to receive God's forgiveness and to become a member of God's family, as the Holy Spirit leads.

Bible Story Recap

On the night before He was arrested, Jesus told Peter that he would deny knowing him three times before the rooster crowed in the morning. Peter loved Jesus so much, he couldn't believe he would EVER deny knowing Jesus!

Then Jesus was arrested. Peter followed when the soldiers took Jesus to the high priest's home for questioning. As he waited in the courtyard, Peter was asked three different times if he knew Jesus. Peter was afraid he would be arrested just for knowing Jesus. All three times, Peter said he didn't know Jesus.

Then the rooster crowed and reminded Peter what Jesus had said. Peter cried bitter tears. He was so sorry he had denied Jesus! Later, after Jesus rose from the tomb, Jesus let Peter know that he had been forgiven.

Teacher's Devotional

It may be easy to judge Peter's actions in today's story by asking, "What was he thinking? Didn't Jesus just warn him that he would deny Him? I would NEVER do that!" Or would you? Peter watched Jesus get arrested, even though He had done nothing wrong. Peter must have been worried about being arrested himself! So yes, Peter denied knowing Jesus. He lied. He was a sinner.

What about you? Aren't you a sinner, too? We all desperately need to be forgiven by Jesus. But not only was Peter forgiven, he was also given a fresh start and commissioned to share Christ's love with others by "feeding His sheep." Jesus is faithful to forgive us (see 1 John 1:9). He won't hold our sins against us (see Psalm 103:9-12).

Consider how precious the gift of forgiveness is for you and receive the fresh start that Christ's forgiveness offers. Pray that your campers will realize their wrong choices, ask Jesus to forgive them and then ask for strength not to repeat the same wrong choices again. Ask Jesus to help you model His forgiveness to the campers in your care.

Lame Man Leaping: Peter Helps a Lame Man

Scripture

Acts 3

Bible Memory Verse

For we are God's workmanship, created in Christ Jesus to do good works, which God prepared in advance for us to do. Ephesians 2:10

Who Am I?

I can live for Jesus and do the good things He has planned for me to do.

Bible Aims for Each Student

During this session, I may

1. TELL that Peter demonstrated Jesus' love and power when he helped the lame man;

2. DISCOVER what Jesus gives to help us live for Him as His children;

3. ASK Jesus to give me strength to live for Him and do the good things He has planned;

4. CHOOSE to receive God's forgiveness and to become a member of God's family, as the Holy Spirit leads.

Bible Story Recap

One day Peter and John were in Jerusalem and de-cided to go to the Temple to pray. There they saw a lame man, who begged them for money. Peter said, "No, I don't have any money to give you," he said. "But what I do have, I give to you! In the name of Jesus, get up and walk!" With Jesus' power, the man was healed!

The man started jumping and running and leaping for joy! When the people in the Temple saw the man, they were amazed. The people thought Peter and John had healed the man. Peter told them the truth. He ex-plained that it was Jesus who had healed the man. Peter was simply doing the good works Jesus had planned for him to do. That day, thousands of people decided to live for Jesus.

Teacher's Devotional

It is hard to see this exciting week come to a close. But for your campers who have chosen to live for Jesus, the excitement is just beginning. Observe their wonder as they discover Jesus' power displayed through Peter, a regular guy, when a lame man is healed! Jesus is the same yesterday, today and tomorrow (see Hebrews 13:8). Just as He allowed Peter to display His power, who knows how He wants to display His power through you and the campers at SonRock Kids Camp!

Think of the ways you have seen the power of Jesus at work this week. When you have shown love to the difficult-to-love child, you have seen God's power at work. When a child or adult has made a decision to live for Jesus, you have seen the power of Jesus at work. When a child has reached out to someone in need, you have seen the power of Jesus at work. As you end the week with your campers, point out the ways you have seen the power of Jesus displayed around SonRock Kids Camp and remind them that God created them with a purpose to do good things (see Ephesians 2:10).

Crafts for Young Children

Craft projects for young children are a blend of "I wanna do it myself!" and "I need help!" Crafts usually require a certain amount of adult assistance—preparing a pattern, doing some cutting, preselecting magazine pictures, tying a knot, etc. But always take care to avoid robbing the child of the satisfaction of his or her own unique efforts. Do only what is absolutely necessary! The adult's desire to have a nice finished project should not override the child's pleasure in experimenting with color, shapes, lines and texture. Avoid the temptation to do the project for the child or to improve on his or her efforts.

Some of these crafts have enrichment and simplification ideas. An enrichment idea provides a way to make the craft more challenging for the older child. A simplification idea helps the younger child complete the craft successfully.

Although most projects in this book allow plenty of leeway for children to be creative, some children may become frustrated with the limitations of a structured craft. This frustration may be a signal that the child needs an opportunity to work with more basic, less structured materials: blank paper and markers, play dough, or precut magazine pictures to make into a collage. In any task a young child undertakes, remember that *the process the child goes through is more important than the finished product*.

Fishing Pole (15-20 MINUTES)

Materials

- Fish Pattern (p. 19)
- brightly-colored masking tape or electrical tape
- twine
- metallic stickers
- colored cellophane cut in small pieces

For each child—

- wrapping paper tube (available for purchase at mailing centers)
- 1-inch (2.5-cm) wood bead
- 2 metal paper clips
- circular magnet with hole in it

Standard Supplies

- white card stock
- scissors
- measuring stick
- hole punch
- markers
- glue sticks

Preparation

Photocopy Fish Pattern onto card stock, two for each child. Cut out. Punch a hole at each end of paper tubes. Cut twine into a 5-feet (1.5-m) length for each child. Tie a large knot in twine 5 inches (12.5 cm) from one end, string wood bead onto twine, then tie that end of twine through one hole in the paper tube (sketch a). Thread the opposite end of twine through the tube and through the hole at the other end of tube. Tie magnet on the end of twine (sketch b). Tear or cut off lengths of colored masking tape or electrical tape and stick ends onto table edge or chair backs, several for each child.

Conversation

Peter was a fisherman. He used nets to catch fish. You can catch fish with your pole. Jesus loved Peter and gave him a new job. Jesus loves you and made you to do good things.

Instruct each child in the following procedures:

- Decorate fish with markers, metallic stickers and/or cellophane pieces.
- Attach paper clips to each fish.
- Wrap brightly colored masking tape on tube to decorate fishing pole.
- Put your fish on the ground and dangle your fishing line over the fish. When you feel the magnet connect to a fish, pull the bead and see if you catch a fish.

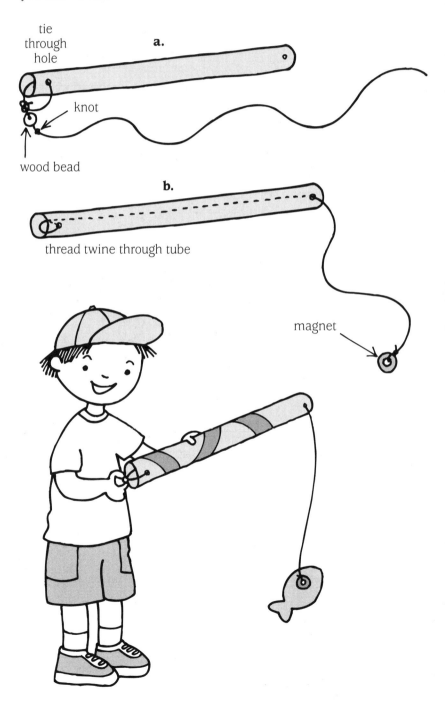

tie through hole

a.

knot

wood bead

b.

thread twine through tube

magnet

Fish Pattern

Cross Necklace (10-15 MINUTES)

Materials

- waxed jute string
- polished rock beads or large wooden beads or plastic beads (wooden beads available from Gospel Light)

For each child—
- wooden cross bead (available from Gospel Light)

Standard Supplies

- scissors
- measuring stick

Preparation

Cut string into 3-feet (.9-m) lengths. Tie a knot in one end of string.

Conversation

Who does your cross necklace remind you of? (Jesus.) **Jesus is God's Son. The Bible says, "Believe in Jesus and that He is alive."**

Instruct each child in the following procedures:

- String half of the beads on the string.
- String on cross.
- String the other half of the beads.
- Teacher (or child) then ties the two ends together.

Enrichment Idea

Children make rock beads out of salt clay or air-drying clay. They use short pieces from bamboo skewers to make holes in beads and allow to dry for a day or two before making necklace. Children can decorate beads with permanent markers.

knot

Fishing Boat Slide (15-20 MINUTES)

Materials

- Boat and Sail Patterns (p. 22)
- blue cellophane
- variety of colored construction paper or card stock
- rocks or pebbles
- craft foam fish shapes 1-inch (2.5-cm) or smaller

For each child—

- blue or white foam tray (used in grocery stores for packaging or available for purchase in stores or through craft supply companies)
- 2 craft sticks

Standard Supplies

- craft knife
- ruler
- scissors
- markers
- low-temp glue gun and glue sticks
- glue

Preparation

Using craft knife, cut a 5-inch (12.5-cm) long slit horizontally across the center of each foam tray (sketch a). Cut cellophane into 2½-inch (6.5-cm) wavy strips the length of the trays, eight for each child. Trace or photocopy Boat Pattern and Sail Pattern onto construction paper or card stock and cut out, one of each for each child. Use glue gun to glue together two craft sticks together to form a "T," one for each child.

Conversation

Kids at camp like to sail in boats. What color boat are you making? Thank you for sharing the glue. You show God's love when you share the glue.

Instruct each child in the following procedures:

- Glue wavy strips on top of foam tray. Do not cover slit.
- Use markers to decorate boat and sail.
- Stick the end of craft stick "T" into slit through the bottom of tray (sketch b).
- Glue boat onto craft stick ½ inch (1.3 cm) above the tray surface (sketch c).
- Glue white sail onto craft stick above boat.
- Glue foam fish and rocks or pebbles onto the cellophane water to decorate the lake.
- Put your hand under the tray and hold the stick. Slide the boat along the slit to make it move. Rock your boat back and forth.

Enrichment Idea

Older children cut out the boat and sail themselves.

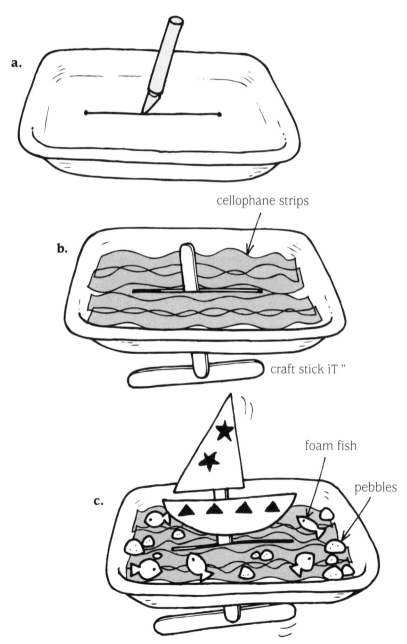

a.

b. cellophane strips

craft stick iT "

c. foam fish

pebbles

Boat and Sail Patterns

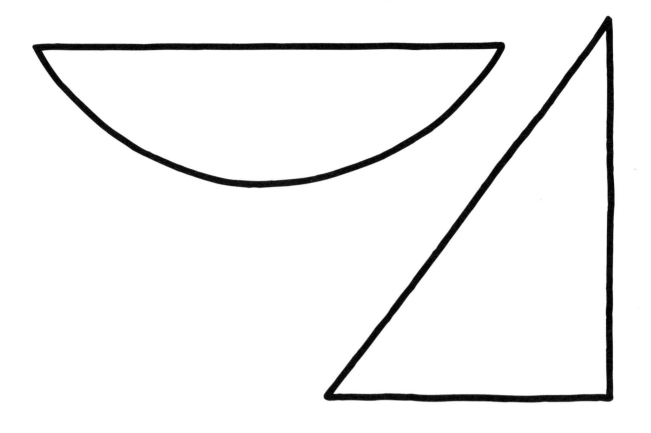

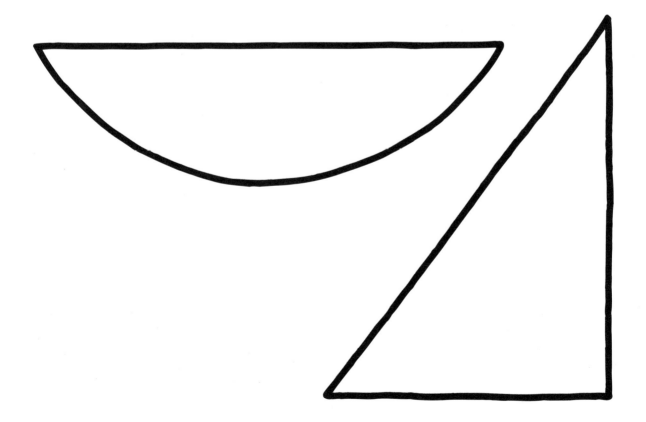

• **Young Children** • **Preschool-Kindergarten** •

Tent Photo Frame (15-20 MINUTES)

Materials

- Tent Patterns (p. 24-25)
- *SonRock Assortment* stickers (available from Gospel Light)
- twine
- self-adhesive magnetic strips

Standard Supplies

- white or tan card stock
- markers
- scissors
- glue

Preparation

One or two days prior to this craft, use a digital camera to photograph and print a 4x6-inch (10x15-cm) picture of each child. Photocopy Tent Patterns onto card stock, one set for each child. Cut out. Cut tent flap slit in center of frame fronts. Bend tent flaps back to reveal opening (sketch a). Cut twine into 4-inch (10-cm) lengths, two for each child.

Conversation

Have you ever slept outside in a tent? You can hear lots of night-time noises when you sleep in a tent. That can be scary. But the Bible tells us, "God says, 'Do not fear; I will help you.'" God's promise is good to remember when we feel scared.

Instruct each child in the following procedures:

- Color tent front with markers. If desired, turn over and color back of tent flaps a different color.
- Glue tent flaps to tent front to keep open.
- Glue photo in center of frame back (sketch b).
- Glue tent frame front on top of frame back with photo revealed through tent flap opening.
- Decorate tent with *SonRock Assortment* stickers.
- Peel off tape from magnetic strips and press strips on the back of frame.
- Teacher punches a hole in each corner tent flap through all card stock layers and ties twine through each hole to make a bow (sketch c).

Enrichment Idea

- Older children cut out Tent Patterns themselves.
- Cut tent fronts out of canvas, nylon, felt or burlap.

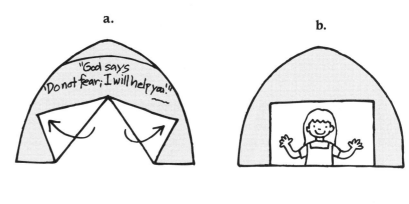

a.

b.

c.

• **Young Children** • **Preschool-Kindergarten** •

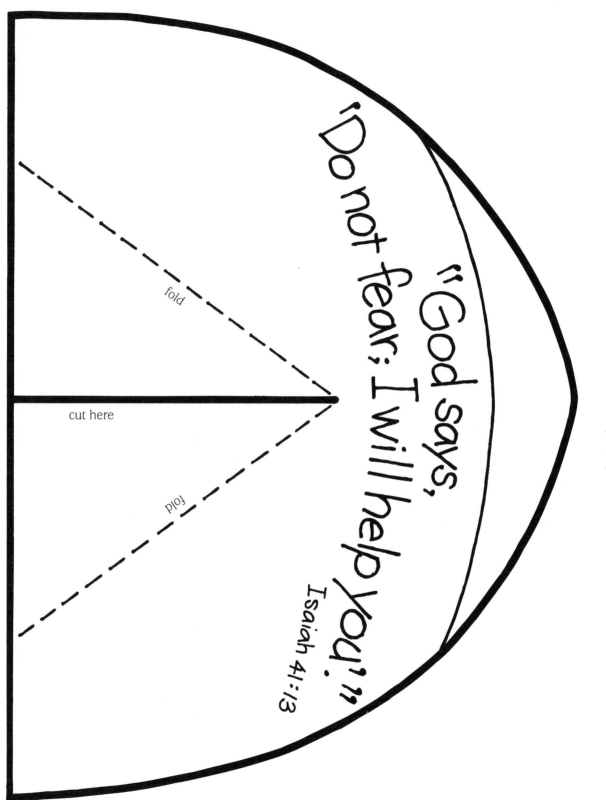

"God says,
'Do not fear; I will help you!'"

Isaiah 41:13

fold

cut here

fold

Tent Pattern (Front)

Tent Pattern (Back)

Forest Friends Puppet (15-20 MINUTES)

Materials

- Forest Friends Puppet Patterns (pp. 27-30)
- lunch-size paper bags (brown for Bear, Moose and Owl; white for skunk and raccoon)
- brown feathers (for Owl)
- colored construction paper or card stock (white, tan, pink, orange)
- wiggle eyes

Optional—

- yarn, felt and fake fur

Standard Supplies

- crayons
- glue

Preparation

Photocopy your choice of Forest Friends Puppet Patterns onto appropriate colors of construction paper or card stock. Prepare enough for each child to make at least one puppet. Cut out pattern pieces.

Conversation

You were kind to share the feathers. What are some other kind things you can do? One kind thing we can do is forgive others. Forgiving means being kind to people who have been mean to us. God forgives us for the wrong things we have done.

Instruct each child in the following procedures:

- Glue mouth or beak under the bag flap (sketch a).
- Color puppet face (and skunk or raccoon tail) to add detail.
- Glue puppet face to paper bag bottom flap (sketch b).
- With crayons, color paper bag body of puppet to make fur. For skunk and raccoon, glue tail to back of puppet so that it sticks out to the side. For owl, glue paper beak pattern to face and feathers to the bag and face. (Optional: Students add texture to puppets by using yarn, felt and fake fur.)

Enrichment Ideas

- Older children cut out the patterns themselves.
- Have a puppet show in your dramatic play center.

Forest Friends Puppet Patterns

Raccoon

Skunk

• **Young Children** • **Preschool-Kindergarten** •

Bear

Owl

• **Young Children • Preschool-Kindergarten** •

Moose Head

• **Young Children** • **Preschool-Kindergarten** •

Forest Friends Puppet Patterns

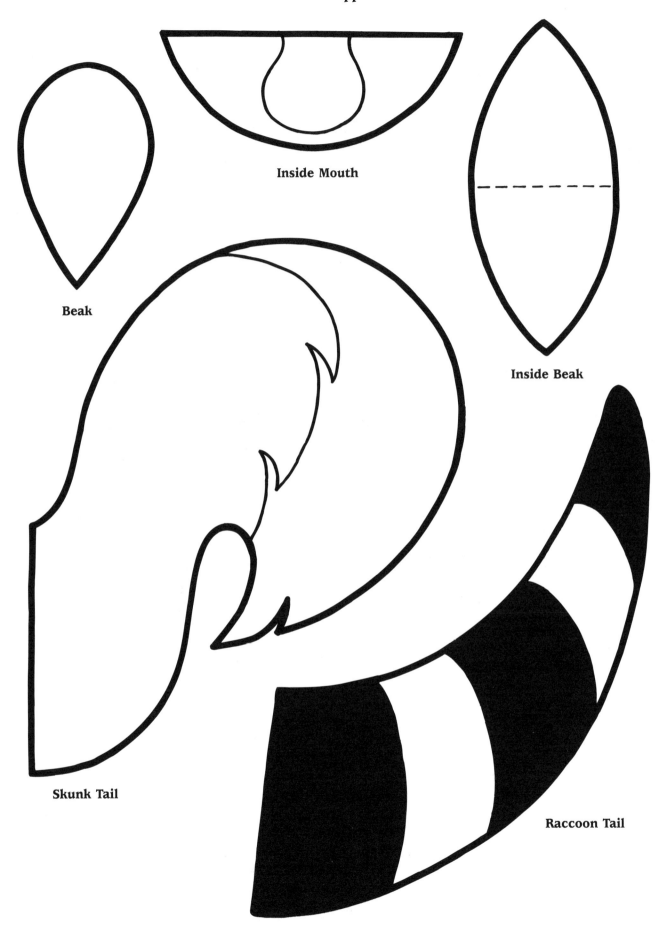

Inside Mouth

Beak

Inside Beak

Skunk Tail

Raccoon Tail

Moose Antlers (10-15 MINUTES)

Materials

- Moose Antler Pattern (p. 32)
- large sheets of brown stiffened felt or craft foam
- $^1/_4$-inch (0.6-cm) ribbon

Standard Supplies

- low-temp glue gun and glue sticks
- craft glue
- hole punch
- fabric scissors
- measuring stick
- small paper clips

Preparation

Cut brown felt into $1^1/_2$x12-inch (4x30.5-cm) strips for headband, one for each child. Punch a hole $^1/_2$ inch (1.3-cm) from each end of headband. With pen, make a mark 3 inches (7.5 cm) from each headband end for antler placement (sketch a). On remainder of brown felt, trace Moose Antler Pattern, four antler patterns for each child. Cut out. Cut ribbon into 20-inch (51-cm) lengths, one for each child.

Conversation

What sound do you think a moose makes? Moose call out when they are lonely or mad. Let's pretend that we are moose. Let's put on our antlers and make our own kind of a moose call. I'm glad God made so many different kinds of animals. God loves us!

Instruct each child in the following procedures:

- Glue two moose antlers together, leaving the bottom $^1/_2$ inch (1.3 cm) unglued. Repeat with the other two antlers.
- With teacher's help, bend the unglued parts of antler open to make flaps (sketch b). Center and glue flaps onto mark on the headband. Put a paper clip over each glued flap to hold until glue dries. Repeat with the other antler.
- Push ribbon end through each hole on the headband and pull through. Teacher knots each ribbon end so ribbon doesn't slip out of holes (sketch c).

Simplification Idea

Purchase foam visors to attach antlers to.

Enrichment Ideas

- Cut brown craft foam in ear shapes and glue moose ears to your headband.
- Children use brown fabric markers, permanent markers or paints to add texture to felt antlers and headband.

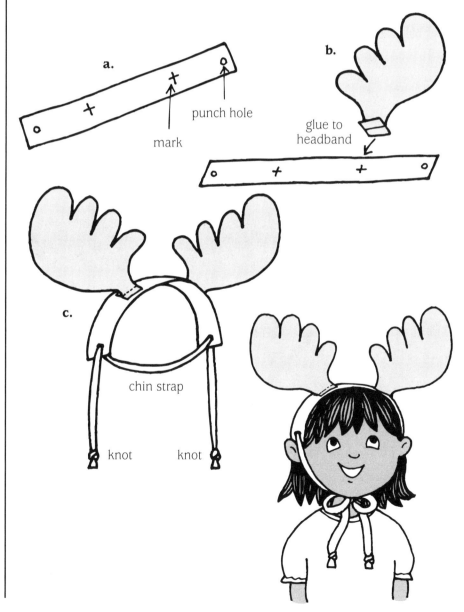

a.

mark

punch hole

b.

glue to headband

c.

chin strap

knot   knot

Moose Antler Pattern

cut four

Peter's Boat-in-a-Bottle (10-15 MINUTES)

Materials

- Boat Pattern
- craft foam
- glitter
- clear iridescent shred
- plastic fish beads (that will fit in the mouth of the water bottle)
- blue food coloring
- address labels

For each child—

- 16.9 oz. plastic water bottle

Standard Supplies

- water
- masking tape or blue duct tape
- pen
- shallow containers

Preparation

Remove labels from bottles. Fill each water bottle with water, stopping about 2 inches (5 cm) from the top of bottle (sketch a). Drop one drop of blue food coloring into each bottle and mix. Trace Boat Pattern on craft foam and cut out, one for each child. With a pen, or a computer, print "Jesus will help _____." on labels and write each child's name on the line on label, one for each child. Place beads, glitter and iridescent shred into shallow containers.

Conversation

Tip the bottle back and forth to make Peter's boat rock. The Bible tells of a time when Peter and his friends were in a boat during a terrible storm. Jesus came and helped them when they were afraid.

Instruct each child in the following procedures:

- Put a pinch of glitter into bottle.
- Stuff some iridescent shred into bottle.
- Drop several beads into bottle.
- Put foam boat shape into bottle.
- Stick label on front of bottle.
- With teacher's help, wrap tape around bottle cap to secure.

a.

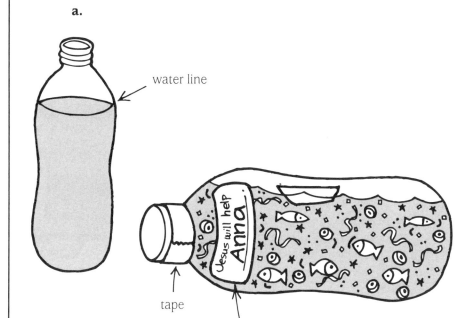

water line

tape

label

Boat Pattern

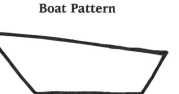

SonRock Backpack (15-20 MINUTES)

Materials

- Sun, Sunray, Tree, Cloud and Hills Patterns (p. 35-36)
- felt in different shades of blue, green, brown, yellow and white
- newspapers or newsprint

For each child—
- drawstring cloth backpack (available from Gospel Light)
- 2 medium-size wiggle eyes

Standard Supplies

- craft glue
- fabric markers

Preparation

Trace Patterns onto appropriate colors of felt and cut out. Make one or more Trees and Clouds for each child. Make one of each Sun, Sunray and Hills pattern for each child. Insert flat folded sheets of newsprint or newspaper inside each backpack so that glue and fabric pens do not bleed through to the back piece of backpack.

Conversation

Backpacks are good to take hiking. What would be a good thing to pack in your backpack? Where will you take your backpack? Wherever we go, we can remember Jesus is with us.

Instruct each child in the following procedures:

- Glue hills on bottom of backpack (sketch a).
- Glue tree(s) on hills.
- Glue sun circle onto sunray piece. Draw smile on sun with marker. Glue wiggle eyes on sun (sketch b). Glue finished sun above the trees in the sky.
- Glue cloud(s) in sky.
- Decorate with fabric markers to add details, if desired.

Enrichment Ideas

- Older students use permanent markers to write a Daily Truth or other phrases about Jesus on the backpack.
- Instead of felt use polar fleece for patterns.

a.

hills

b.

wiggle eyes

draw on smile

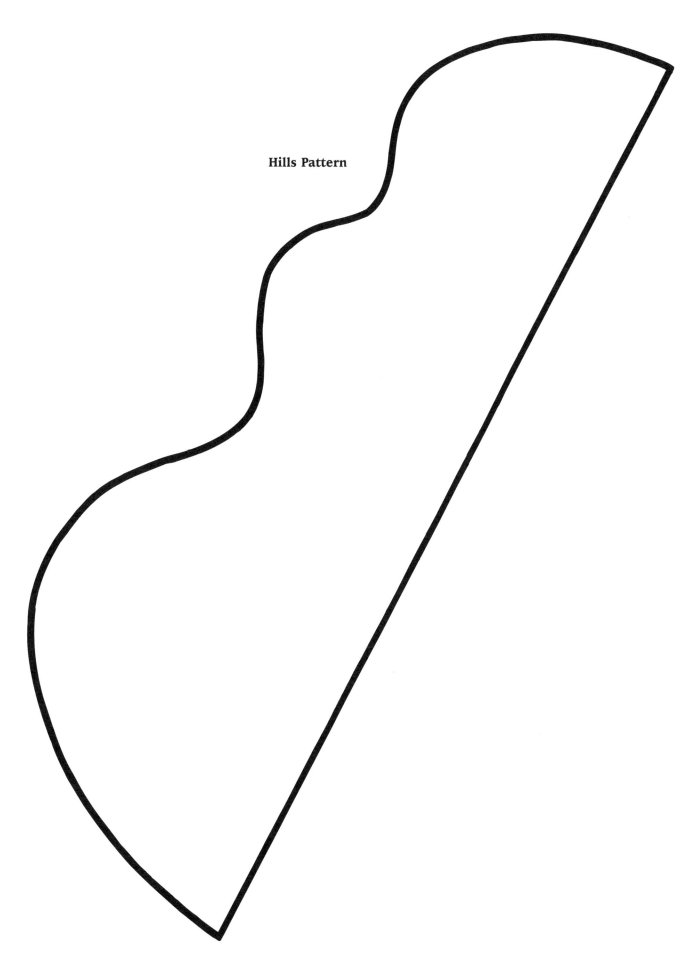

Hills Pattern

Cloud Pattern

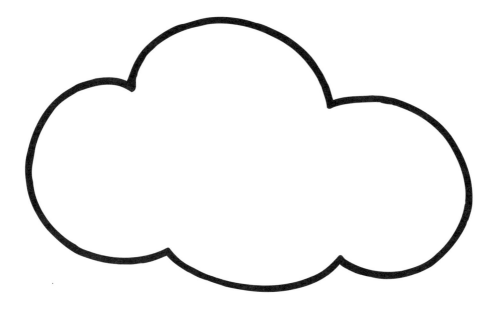

Sunray Pattern

Tree Pattern

Sun Pattern

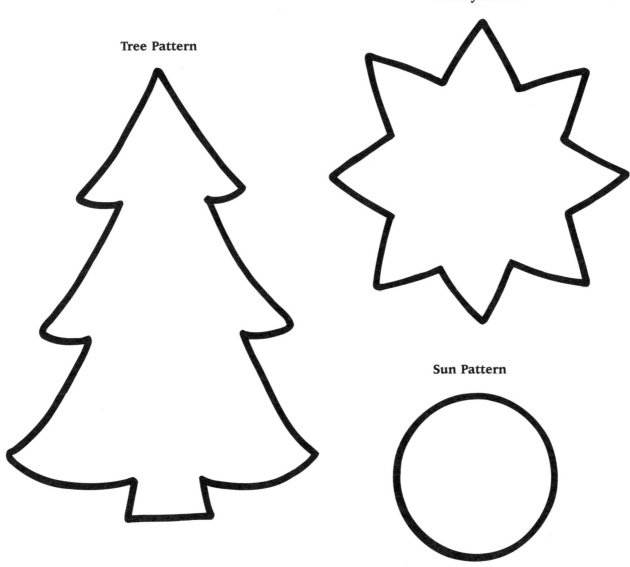

Trail Tracks Banner (15-20 MINUTES)

Materials

- Rock, Grass, Lizard Patterns (p. 38)
- felt in green, brown, grey
- craft foam or felt bug shapes
- yarn or raffia

For each child—

- One 12-inch (30.5-cm) wood dowel
- 1 tan 9x12-inch (23x30.5-cm) felt sheet

Standard Supplies

- pen
- fabric scissors
- low-temp glue gun and glue sticks
- brightly colored card stock
- hole punch
- markers

Preparation

Trace patterns onto appropriate colors of felt. For each child make one lizard, four to six rocks, and four to six grass pieces. Cut out all felt pieces. Use glue gun to glue a wood dowel across one edge of each tan felt sheet. Cut raffia or yarn into 20-inch (51-cm) lengths. Cut the card stock into 3x5-inch (7.5x12.5-cm) cards. With marker, print "I was made to do good things." on the cards, one for each child (or use computer and printer to print words on card stock, and then cut apart). Punch two holes near the top of each card.

Conversation

You can hang your Trail Tracks Banner in your room. What will you think of when you see your banner? All the animals, rocks and even your own footprints on your banner can remind you that God made all things! And He made you to do good things.

Instruct each child in the following procedures:

- Ask a teacher to use a trace around your foot or shoe with a pen.
- Outline your footprint with a marker.
- Glue rock and grass felt pieces along the long edges of banner to make the edges of path (sketch a).
- Glue felt lizard and bug shapes onto banner.
- Push yarn or raffia through both holes in the card. Pull card to the center of yarn or raffia.
- Teacher ties ends of yarn or raffia to each end of dowel at top of banner to make hanger (sketch b).

Simplification Idea

Trace Footprint Pattern (p. 39) onto felt and cut out, making one for each child. Child glues footprint on banner, instead of making own footprint.

Enrichment Idea

Instead of using tan felt for banner, use a sheet of sandpaper. Instead of felt for rocks, child crumples brown or grey construction paper to make rocks and glues to the sides of path. Instead of felt grass, child cuts green strips of construction paper into fringe for grass, or use shredded green paper. Glue in between rocks. Punch holes at top of banner and use yarn or raffia to tie the banner onto the dowel.

Lizard Pattern

Rock Patterns

Grass Patterns

Footprint Pattern

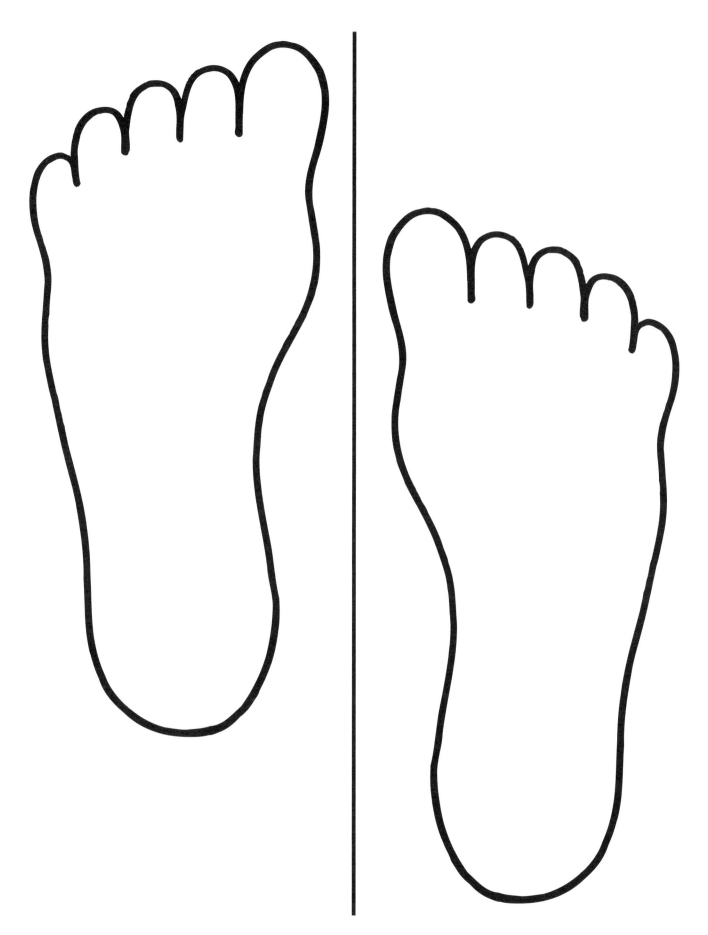

Nature Journal (10-15 MINUTES)

Materials

- 12x18-inch (30.5x45.5-cm) craft foam sheets in a variety of colors
- Con-Tact® paper
- leaves, flowers, grasses
- double-stick tape
- 1-inch (2.5-cm) paper fasteners (brads)
- permanent markers or paint pens

Standard Supplies

- paper
- card stock
- ruler
- scissors
- hole punch

Preparation

To make journal covers, cut foam sheets into fourths, two 6x9-inch (15x23-cm) rectangles for each child. Cut a 3½x6-inch (9x15-cm) window out of half the foam rectangles for the journal front cover (sketch a). Cut card stock and Con-Tact paper into 5x8-inch (12.5x20.5-cm) rectangles, one of each for each child. Cut paper in half to make approximately 10 pages for each child. Punch three holes in left hand side of each foam front and back cover so that they line up (sketch d). Punch corresponding holes in paper pages.

Conversation

What plants will you use for your Nature Journal? What is your favorite plant? God made all the wonderful plants for us to enjoy because He loves us.

Instruct each child in the following procedures:

- With teacher's help, peel backing off Con-Tact paper and lay flat, sticky side up. Place several nature items (leaves, flowers, grass) facedown onto sticky surface to make collage.
- With teacher's help, place card stock piece on top of Con-Tact paper. Turn over and smooth the Con-Tact paper down, around the nature items. Press pieces together to seal (sketch b).
- Place pieces of double-sided tape along edges of the Con-Tact paper side of nature collage. Center foam journal cover over collage and press together so that collage shows through the window (sketch c).
- Put paper between the front and back covers and push paper fasteners through holes. Open prongs to secure.
- Write name, or teacher writes name, on front of journal with permanent markers or paint pens (sketch d).

Simplification Idea

Before class, teacher assembles journals. Children only assemble the nature collage window and add to journal cover.

Enrichment Ideas

- Insert *My Camp Journal* into journal or use reproducible journal pages from *Camp Décor and More*.
- Take children on a nature walk to collect nature items before craft.
- Children sew journal together with twine or yarn. Add pony beads to the ends of the twine or yarn and tie securely.

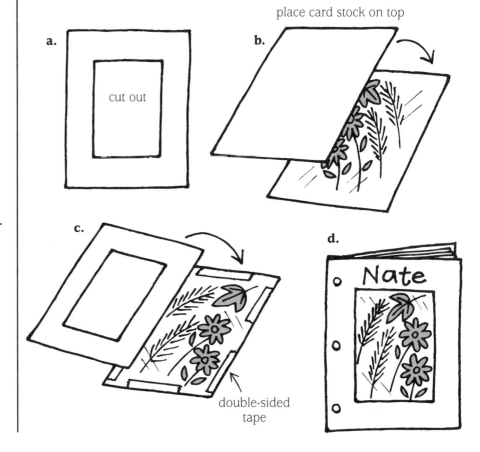

a. cut out

b. place card stock on top

c.

d. Nate

double-sided tape

Camp Cabin Bank (20-25 MINUTES)

Materials

- construction paper, in a variety of colors including brown
- flower and plant stickers

For each child—

- One 4-inch (10-cm) Chinese food take-out box

Standard Supplies

- craft knife
- scissors
- tape
- markers
- glue

Preparation

Cut brown paper into 4-inch (10-cm) squares—four for each child. For each child, use additional colors of construction paper to cut out a 4x9-inch (10x23-cm) rectangle for roof piece, a 2x3-inch (5x7.5-cm) rectangle for door and two 2-inch (5-cm) squares for windows. Fold roof pieces where indicated in sketch a. Near the top of the front of the box use craft knife to cut out a slot large enough for a quarter to fit through. Tape the lid of the box closed (sketch b).

Conversation

What will you do with the money you save in your Camp Cabin Bank? When your bank is full, have your mommy or daddy cut out the door. You can empty all the money you have saved and use it to do **something good!** (Optional: Suggest children use bank to save money for your church's mission project.)

Instruct each child in the following procedures:

- Glue a brown paper square to one side of box. Wrap paper around corner edges and glue to sides. Cut slits in paper to fit around handles (sketch c).
- Continue gluing brown paper squares to each side of box.
- Teacher cuts away brown paper from coin slot.
- Glue the largest section of roof piece to the top of box. Then bend the rest of piece to make a pointed roof and glue the opposite end to the top edge (sketch d).
- Use markers to draw details (doorknob, windowpanes, curtains) on windows and door.
- Glue door to front of box, under the coin slot.
- Glue windows on either side of cabin.
- Place flower and plant stickers on the bottom edge of cabin.

Simplification Idea

Purchase brown take-out boxes (available at craft suppliers) or cover all boxes with paper beforehand.

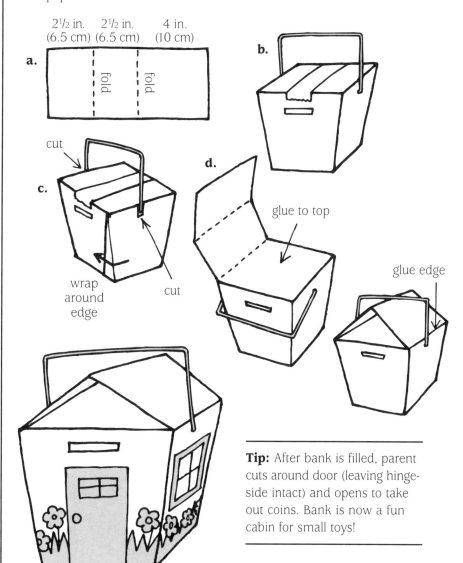

Tip: After bank is filled, parent cuts around door (leaving hinge-side intact) and opens to take out coins. Bank is now a fun cabin for small toys!

Stepping Stone (10-15 MINUTES)

Materials

- quick-dry mortar
- medium-sized plastic tub
- short hoe or hand spade
- paint stick
- nature items (seedpods, small pinecones, rocks, pebbles, leaves, twigs)
- mosiac tiles or glass pebbles

For each child—

- 8-inch (20.5-cm) plastic plant pot saucer (available in the garden section of home improvement or discount stores) or aluminum pie pan

Standard Supplies

- water

Preparation

Using hoe or hand spade, mix mortar and water in tub as directed on packaging. Mortar dries quickly, so only mix what you will use for each group of children. Pour prepared mortar into each saucer or pan.

Conversation

You can put your stepping stone in your garden at home. It can remind you of all the fun you had at SonRock Kids Camp. What are some things you have learned about and done this week?

Instruct each child in the following procedures:

- Use paint stick to press mortar in saucer or pan to make the stepping stone smooth and level (sketch a).
- Press nature items, mosaic tiles and/or glass pebbles into mortar to decorate.
- Let dry overnight.
- Remove stepping stone from saucer or pan.

a.   smooth mortar

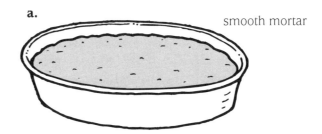

Flying Forest Bird (15-20 MINUTES)

Materials

- Bird and Wing Patterns (p. 44)
- card stock in a variety of colors
- construction paper in a variety of colors
- small feathers in a variety of colors

For each child—
- 5-inch (12.5-cm) cardboard tube

Standard Supplies

- scissors
- ruler
- crayons
- glue

Preparation

For bird body, fold card stock in half, and then lay Bird Pattern on fold where indicated (sketch a). Trace or photocopy Bird and Wing Patterns onto card stock, one Bird Pattern and two Wing Patterns for each child. Cut out. On the straight edge of each wing, fold over a ½-inch (1.3-cm) tab. Cut construction paper into 4½x6-inch (11.5x15-cm) rectangles, one for each child.

Conversation

Birds can fly high in the sky. Can you make your bird's wings flap? Where do birds make their homes? Have you ever seen a bird's nest? God made the birds so they would know how to build their nests. We can see so many wonderful things that God made. God loves us!

Instruct each child in the following procedures:

- Glue feathers onto wings.
- Spread glue on construction-paper rectangle. Lay paper tube on the rectangle and wrap the paper around the tube to cover (sketch b).
- Use crayons to color bird beak and eyes on both sides of head.
- With scissors, cut tail fringe to make tail feathers (sketch c).
- With teacher's help, glue folded tab of wings onto paper tube about ½ inch (1.3 cm) apart (sketch d).
- Spread glue onto paper tube below each wing. Hold the wings together while teacher slips bird body over wings and onto the paper tube (sketch e).
- Put your finger into tube and move bird up and down to make bird fly.

Simplification Idea
Cover paper tubes with construction paper beforehand.

Enrichment Ideas
- Older children may cut out patterns.
- Give each pair of children a 15- to 20-foot (4.5- to 6-m) length of nylon string. Children thread string through cardboard tube. Each child holds one end of string and stands far apart, holding string taut. One child holds string high and one holds string low to make bird "fly" across the room.

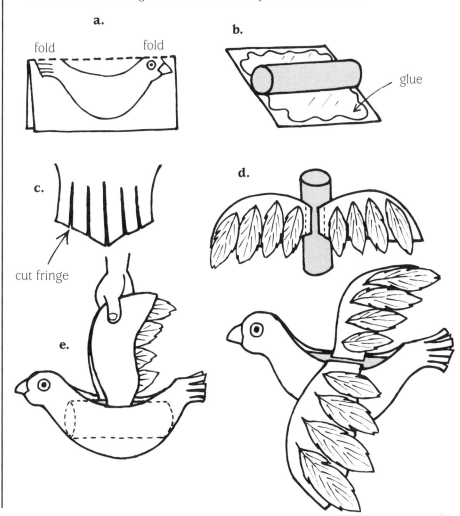

a.   fold   fold

b.   glue

c.   cut fringe

d.

e.

Flying Forest Bird Patterns

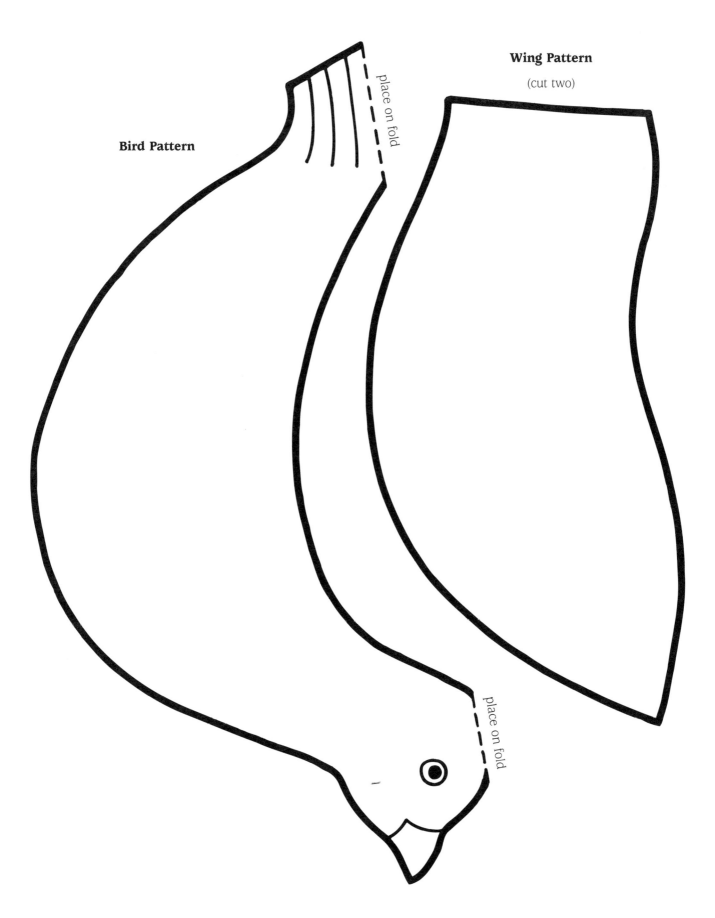

Bird Pattern

Wing Pattern

(cut two)

place on fold

place on fold

• *Young Children* • **Preschool-Kindergarten** •

Fishing Hat (10-15 MINUTES)

Materials

- sponges
- spring-type clothespins
- acrylic fabric paints in a variety of colors
- feathers in a variety of colors
- wood beads (8- to 10-mm)

For each child—

- white child-size bucket hat (available at craft stores or online craft supply sites)
- paint smock or adult T-shirt to protect clothing
- two or three large safety pins

Standard Supplies

- disposable Styrofoam or plastic plates
- scissors
- transparent tape

Preparation

Cut sponges into 2-inch (5-cm) pieces. Dampen sponges and clip a clothespin to each sponge piece to make a handle (sketch a). Pour paints into separate disposable plates and place one or more sponge brush onto each plate. Begin making two or more "fishing lures" for each child: Hold two or more feather quills together and wrap with a short piece of tape to secure together. Open each safety pin and pierce the taped portion of feather quills with the pin, stringing them onto the safety pin shaft (sketch b).

Conversation

Fishermen wear hats to protect them from getting too much sun. Our Bible tells us about a man named Peter. Peter was a fisherman. Jesus loved Peter and wanted him to be His friend. Jesus loves us and wants us to be His friends, too.

Instruct each child in the following procedures:

- Hold clothespin handle and dip sponge into paint. Dab on the hat in several places. Then choose another color to paint on hat. Continue sponge painting, using desired colors, until hat is covered. Allow plenty of white cloth to still show through painting (sketch c).
- Finish making two or three lures with feathers, beads and safety pins. With teacher's help and supervision, open safety pins, string wood beads onto the pin shafts and close safety pins (sketch d).
- After hat is dry, teacher pins lures onto hat.
- Now you are ready to go fishing!

Simplification Ideas

- Use fabric markers or permanent markers to decorate hats.
- Make lures in advance and invite children to choose one they would like.

a.

b.

tape

c.

d.

Critter Box (10-15 MINUTES)

Materials

- window screening
- colored duct tape
- garden or nature stickers (grass, flowers, rocks, lizards, bugs)
- craft foam stickers (grass, flowers, rocks, lizards, bugs)
- colored permanent markers

For each child—
- clear plastic container with lid
- several plastic bugs (available from Gospel Light)

Standard Supplies

- craft knife
- ruler
- sharp scissors

Preparation

Using craft knife cut a 3x6-inch (7.5x15-cm) rectangle in the center of each lid. Using scissors cut window screening into 4x7-inch (10x18-cm) rectangles, one for each lid. Cut lengths of duct tape to make a border around the cut-out of each lid. Wrap the tape to the inside to cover the cut edges of plastic (sketch a). Tape the screening to the inside of lids over the opening (sketch b). On top of each lid, use permanent marker to write "_____'s Critters." Make line and space large enough for preschooler to write name.

Conversation

We created a fun Critter Box for our toy bugs. God made bugs to do special jobs. Ladybugs eat little green bugs, called aphids, that bother pretty roses. That is good thing for ladybugs to do. God made us to do good things!

Instruct each child in the following procedures:

- Write your name above the line on the lid (sketch c).
- Decorate the sides of your Critter Box with stickers.
- Use markers to add other details to the sides of box (sketch d).
- Choose bugs to live in your Critter Box.

Enrichment Idea
Provide nature items (dirt, sand, grass, twigs and leaves) to put in their Critter Box.

a.

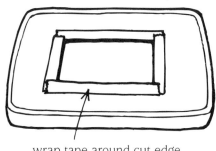

wrap tape around cut edge

b.

window screen

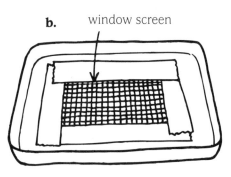

c.

d.

Crafts for Younger Elementary

Children in the first few years of school delight in completing craft projects. They have a handle on most of the basic skills needed, they are eager to participate, and their taste in art has usually not yet surpassed their ability to produce. In other words, they generally like what they make.

Because reading ability is not a factor in most craft projects, crafts can be a great leveler among children. Some children who are not top achievers in other areas excel here.

You may find additional projects suitable for younger elementary children in the first section of this book, "Crafts for Young Children."

Leaf Print Journal

(ONE- OR TWO-DAY CRAFT—20-25 MINUTES TOTAL TIME)

Materials

- small to medium sized nature items for printing (leaves, seeds, pods, halved mushrooms, etc.)
- corrugated cardboard
- acrylic paints (preferably shades of green, brown, gold, orange, etc.)
- clear Con-Tact® paper
- paper fasteners (brads)

For each child—

- 1 9x12-inch (23x30.5-cm) sheet of 140 lb/300 gsm weight (or greater) watercolor paper
- 1 or more pressed, dried flowers or/and leaves

Standard Supplies

- hole punch
- heavy-duty scissors
- sponge brushes
- paper
- paper cutter
- glue
- shallow containers
- ruler

Preparation

Fold each sheet of watercolor paper in half for journal cover. Punch three evenly-spaced holes in the fold side of each cover (sketch a). Cut copier paper in half for journal pages—10 to 20 pages for each child. Punch holes in pages to correspond with holes in journal cover. Cut cardboard into pieces larger than nature item. Glue items to cardboard pieces to make stamps (sketch b). (Tip: If making Tree Shirt save nature stamps.) Chunkier items, such as halved mushrooms or large seeds, do not need to be glued to cardboard. Pour paints in separate shallow containers. Cut clear Con-Tact paper into 3½-inch (9-cm) squares—two for each child.

Instruct each child in the following procedures:

- Peel away backing from one Con-Tact paper square and center it on the front of journal cover. Press in place, lightly. Open cover and lay flat on the table, with the front facing up (sketch c).
- Choose a nature stamp item. Lightly brush the item with paint. Press onto cover in several places. Repeat with the same stamp and color, if desired.
- Choose a different stamp and paint with a different color. Press to make design on cover. Repeat with other items and paint, as desired (sketch d).
- As you work, stamp around the edges of the Con-Tact paper square and overlap it. Allow paints to dry.
- Carefully remove the Con-Tact paper square to reveal the unpainted square underneath (sketch e).
- Choose one or more pressed dried flowers and/or leaves and arrange on the square area.
- Peel the backing from the remaining Con-Tact paper square. Center it over the pressed flowers and/or leaves and smooth it onto the cover, pressing down secure all around the pressed items (sketch f).
- Place 10 sheets of punched paper inside the journal and line up holes with the journal cover holes.
- Place a paper fastener through each hole and secure pages in book (sketch g).

Simplification Idea

Use *SonRock Assortment stickers* (available from Gospel Light) or nature stamps instead of real nature items.

Enrichment Ideas

- Store *My Camp Journals* during VBS. On the last day, punch and insert pages into journal with the additional blank pages.
- Use a marker or paint pen to print a title on the journal cover after paint has dried.
- Sew journals together with twine, jute or yarn and provide beads to tie on to the ends.
- Instead of using pressed flowers, personalize the journal by placing a child's picture in the center of the journal cover.

Conversation

What will you write in your journal? You can write about the people that you love. You can write about your day at VBS. You can write about your favorite things. You can also write down what you'd like to say to God. The Bible says, *You are forgiving and good, O Lord, abounding in love to all who call to you"* (Psalm 86:5). We call to God when we pray aloud and when we pray silently. You can even call to God when you write your prayer in your journal. God always listens.

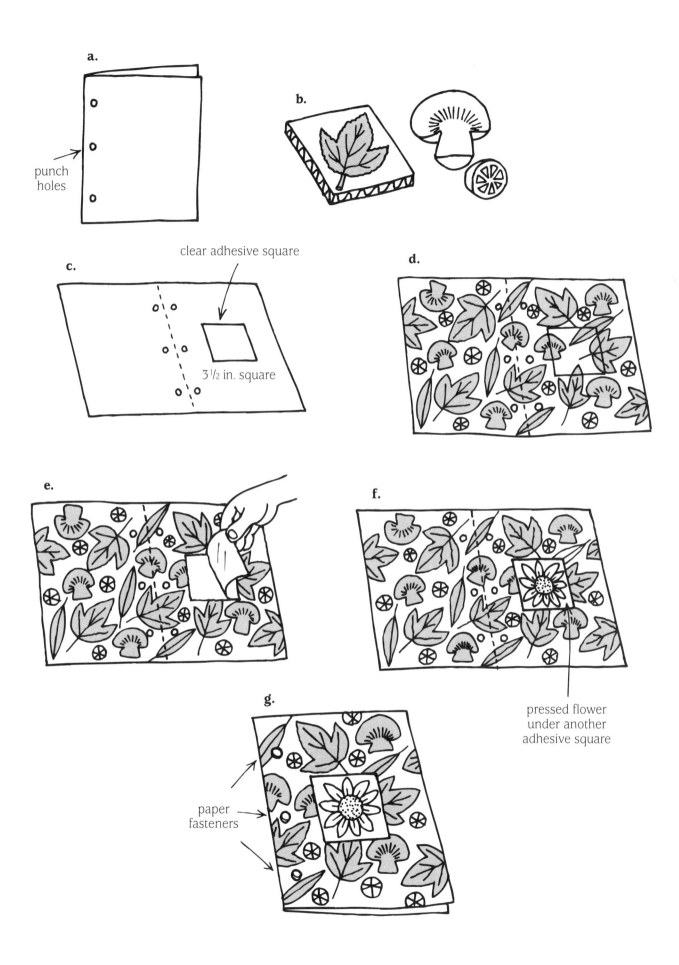

a.

punch holes

b.

c.

clear adhesive square

3 1/2 in. square

d.

e.

f.

pressed flower under another adhesive square

g.

paper fasteners

Rockin' Pendant (15 MINUTES)

Materials

- steel, brass or copper wire (20 gauge)
- wire cutters
- leather lacing
- needle-nose pliers

For each child—

- 1 small rock approximately 1-inch (2.5-cm) in diameter

Standard Supplies

- measuring stick
- heavy-duty scissors

Preparation

Use wire cutters to cut an 18-inch (45.5-cm) length of wire and heavy-duty scissors to cut a 2-foot (61-cm) length of leather lacing for each child.

Conversation

What does your rock feel like? It is hard. Could you crush it with your hands? A rock is firm. Jesus is sometimes referred to as the rock on which we build our lives. He is a firm foundation for us. When you wear your Rockin' Pendant, remember how much Jesus loves you and wants you to depend on Him.

Instruct each child in the following procedures:

- Lay the rock in the center of the wire (sketch a). Bring both sides of the wire around the rock to meet. Twist wire together right next to the rock to secure the rock inside (sketch b).
- Wrap each end of the wire around the rock in various directions several times, holding wire close to the rock. Twist the wires together one or two times while wrapping. Stop when you have 3 to 4 inches (7.5 to 10 cm) at the end of each wire.
- Bring wires together at the top of the rock pendant and twist together (sketch c). Continue twisting the wires together, and then bend the twisted wire into a loop. Twist the wires around the base of the loop to form an opening for the lacing (sketch d). It may help to form the loop over a pencil using pliers.
- Teacher cuts off excess wire with wire cutters and uses pliers to crimp sharp wire ends and secure the loop closing.
- Thread leather lacing through the wire loop of the rock pendant.
- Hold both ends of leather lacing together. Tie an overhand knot near the ends (sketch e).

Enrichment Idea

Children string four or five small stone or shell beads onto wire before they begin wrapping rock.

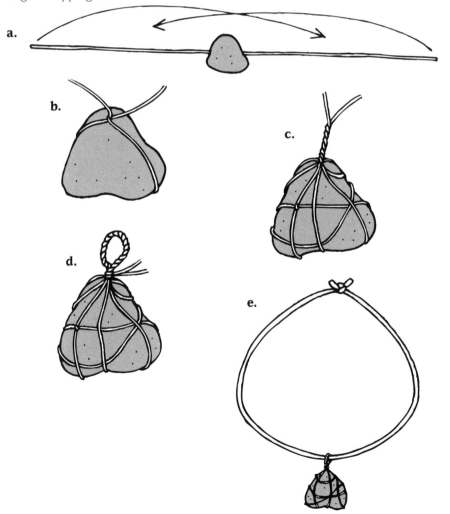

Camp Canteen (TWO-DAY CRAFT/20-25 MINUTES TOTAL TIME)

Materials

- adhesive-backed craft foam sheets in various colors
- small craft foam shapes
- squeeze bottles of fabric paint
- 1-inch (2.5-cm) wide grosgrain ribbon

For each child—

- 20 oz. bottle of water with straight sides

Standard Supplies

- craft glue or craft glue dots
- scissors
- masking tape
- measuring stick

Conversation

You can use your canteen to carry water on a hike. **Why is it important when you go on outdoor adventures to carry water with you?** (You might get lost. You might be gone longer than you thought you would. You need water for your body to work properly.) There are many ways we can be safe when we are out in the wilderness. **What are some other things that will keep you safe when you are hiking or swimming in the mountains?** Children respond. Jesus gives us (parents, equipment, knowledge) to help take care of us wherever we are. The Bible says, *Do not fear; I will help you* (Isaiah 41:13).

Day One Preparation

Cut craft foam sheets into rectangles the size of water bottle labels—one rectangle for each water bottle.

Instruct each child in the following procedures:

- Write name on rectangle with squeeze paints. Glue foam shapes onto craft foam rectangle to decorate. Use squeeze paints to make dots, squiggles, and/or zig-zag designs, if desired (sketch a).
- Allow to dry overnight.

Day Two Preparation

Cut ribbon into 40-inch (101.5 cm) lengths—one for each child.

Instruct each child in the following procedures:

- Lay ribbon flat on table. Set water bottle in the center point of the ribbon. Hold ribbon ends straight up above the water bottle, with ribbon flat against each side of water bottle to make sure ends are even (sketch b).
- Lay ribbon ends back on table. Squeeze craft glue onto the ribbon that will run along the sides of the bottle and then smooth the ribbon up the bottle on each side (sketch c).
- Hold the ribbons tight to the top of the bottle while a partner or teacher tapes the ribbon in place on the sides and to the bottle top (sketch d).
- Ask a partner to hold the ribbon above the bottle, out of the way. Remove backing from the decorated craft foam rectangle, and wrap the decorated foam rectangle around the bottle, centering the name between the ribbon. Press foam label firmly in place (sketch e).
- Hold the ribbon ends together and tie in an overhand knot. Pull firmly to make sure the knot is tight.
- Remove the tape from around bottle top and ribbon.
- Wear your Camp Canteen over your shoulder as you go on your adventures!

Simplification Idea

To make this a one-day craft use permanent markers or paint pens to write name and draw designs on foam, instead of squeeze paints.

Enrichment Idea

Tie plastic lacing around the neck of the bottle and string pony beads onto ends for colorful dangles.

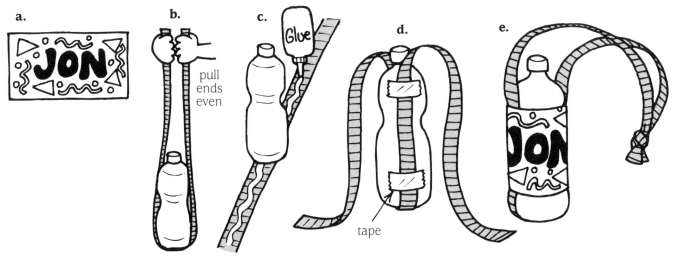

a.   b. pull ends even   c. Glue   d. tape   e.

Live for Jesus Calendar (20-25 MINUTES)

Materials

- colored poster board
- large nature photos from discarded wall calendars or magazine pictures
- nature items (pressed leaves, dried moss, seeds, pods, etc.)
- twine

For each child—
- 1 tree twig 14 inches (35.5-cm) long

Standard Supplies

- measuring stick
- paper
- computer, calendar software and printer
- markers
- scissors
- craft glue
- colored card stock
- stapler and staples
- hole punch

Preparation

Cut large sheets of poster board in half widthwise, one half for each child. Remove calendar pages from calendars and trim any ragged edges or gather magazine pictures. Cut twine into 2-foot (61-cm) lengths, two for each child. Cut colored card stock into 2x11-inch (5x28-cm) strips, two for each child. Use computer and calendar software to print out calendar pages, one set of 12 monthly pages for each child. Arrange calendar pages in order, with the current month on top. Staple together in three places along the top of calendar pages.

Instruct each child in the following procedures:

- Glue a card stock strip to the top edge of back of calendar pages. Then glue the strip to the poster board positioning the pages in the bottom half of poster board (sketch a).
- Choose a nature photo or magazine picture for your calendar. Glue it to the top portion of the poster board.
- Punch a hole near each top corner of the poster board, about 1 or 2 inches (2.5 or 5 cm) from the outside edge (sketch b).
- Tie center of one twine length around the twig about 1 or 2 inches (2.5 or 5 cm) from each end. Knot. Repeat with other twine length on the opposite end of twig (sketch c).
- Place the twig across the top of poster board. On one side, hold strands together and thread the twine through punched hole. Repeat with the twine on the opposite end of stick (sketch d).
- Gather all the twine strands together and tie in an overhand knot to complete calendar hanger.
- On another card stock strip, use markers to print, "Live for Jesus Every Day." Glue onto calendar.
- Glue a few pressed leaves or other nature items onto poster board borders around picture and calendar pages (sketch e).

Simplification Idea

Eliminate twig hanger and simply punch a hole in the top center of calendar to hang.

Enrichment Ideas

- Give children Christian symbol stickers to place on Sundays to remind them about Sunday School attendance. Give children various holiday stickers to use on calendar.
- Cut squares or rectangles out of card stock. Children glue the bottom and side edges of the card stock to the back of calendar to make a pocket to hold stickers.
- Mark the dates of next year's VBS on the calendar.

Conversation

Jesus gives us the strength to do good things every day. Your calendar can help you remember to live every day of the week as Jesus wants you to. What is something good you could do on a day you go to school? On a summer day? On the weekend with your family or friends? Jesus has all kinds of good things planned for you to do every day. The Bible says, *For we are God's workmanship, created in Christ Jesus to do good works* (Ephesians 2:10).

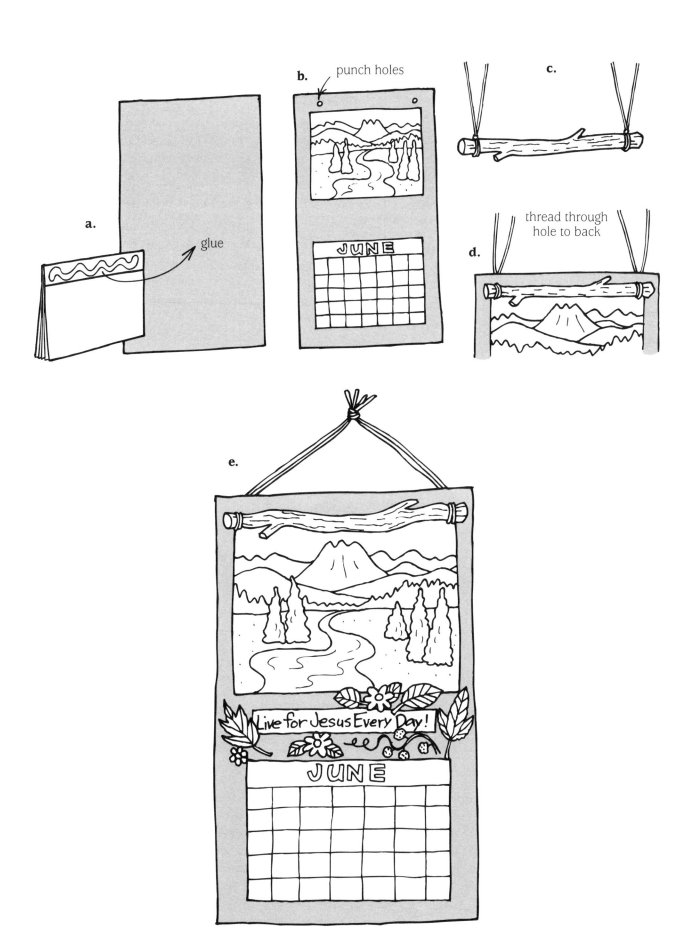

a.

glue

b. punch holes

c.

d. thread through hole to back

e.

Live for Jesus Every Day!

JUNE

Tree Shirt (20-25 MINUTES)

Materials

- Leaf and Tree Patterns (see p. 56-58)
- nature items for printing (flattened leaves, pine needles, pinecones, seed pods, dried moss, bark, halved mushrooms purchased at store, etc.) Tip: Use the stamps created for the Leaf Print Journal craft.
- fabric paints in various colors
- corrugated cardboard
- clear Con-Tact® paper

For each child—

- 1 T-shirt

Standard Supplies

- heavy-duty scissors
- craft glue
- shallow containers
- lightweight cardboard
- newspapers
- foam brushes
- ballpoint pens
- scissors

Preparation

Cut cardboard into pieces larger than nature items. Glue leaves, pine needles, seed pods and moss to separate cardboard pieces to make stamps for children to share (sketch a). Chunkier items, such as halved mushrooms or large seeds, do not need to be glued to cardboard. Pour paints into containers. Trace Leaf and Tree patterns onto lightweight cardboard and cut out. Make several of each pattern. Cut Con-Tact paper into 7x12-inch (18x30.5-cm) sized pieces for children to trace patterns onto.

Instruct each child in the following procedures:

- Use a pen to trace one or more leaf or tree patterns onto the paper backing of Con-Tact paper. Cut out patterns.
- Slide folded newspaper inside t-shirt so that it lies flat.
- Peel backing off Con-Tact patterns and arrange on front of t-shirt, pressing edges down firmly (sketch b).
- Choose a nature stamp. Brush item with paint (sketch c). Press down onto shirt several times.
- Continue stamping with various colors and stamps, making sure to stamp over the edges of the Con-Tact paper patterns so the shapes will appear when patterns are removed.
- Allow shirts to dry.
- Remove Con-Tact paper patterns (sketch e).

Tip: After painting, the mottled appearance of the adhesive leaf and tree patterns make attractive window clings. Give each child a sheet of wax paper to place their leaf and tree shapes on after they remove them from their shirts to take home.

Simplification Idea

Use cut sponges instead of nature stamps, or eliminate the Con-Tact paper patterns and only stamp with nature items.

Enrichment Ideas

- After removing leaf or tree Con-Tact paper patterns, use a permanent marker or fabric pen to outline the resulting shapes on the T-shirt.
- Using colorful permanent markers, older children can write Daily Truths around design.

Conversation

What do trees need in order to live? (Water, air, soil, sunshine.) **What do you need to live?** (Water, air, food, etc.) God made a way so that we can live, not only here on earth, but forever! He sent Jesus to die and live again so, if we believe that Jesus is God's Son, we can have eternal life. When you wear your Tree Shirt, you can remember the gifts Jesus gives us. The Bible says, *If you confess with your mouth, 'Jesus is Lord,' . . . you will be saved* (Romans 10:9).

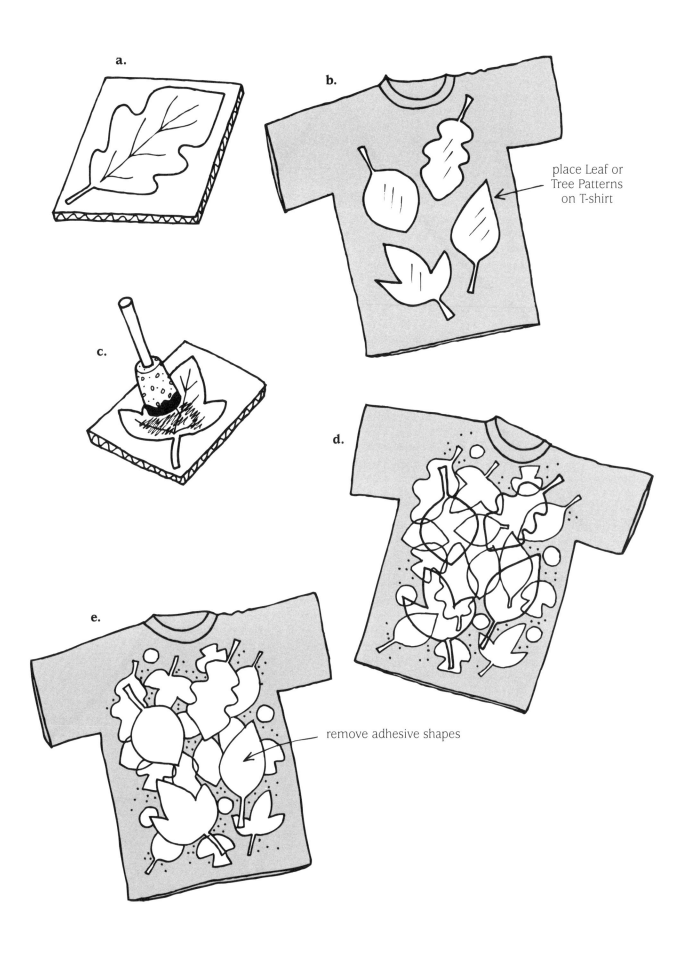

a.

b.

place Leaf or
Tree Patterns
on T-shirt

c.

d.

e.

remove adhesive shapes

Pine Tree Pattern

Tree Pattern

Leaf Patterns

Rugged Cross (20-25 MINUTES)

Materials

- terra cotta air-drying clay
- various nature items (pine needles, small pine cones, acorns, small seed pods, sturdy dried leaves)
- plastic forks

Standard Supplies

- small paper clips
- knife
- newspaper
- water
- shallow containers
- paper plates

Preparation

Cut clay into 2-inch (5-cm) cubes—one for each child. Cover work area with layers of newspaper. Fill shallow containers with water. Distribute a paper plate to each child to carry his or her cross home to dry on.

Conversation

In our Bible story, Peter felt bad that he said he didn't know Jesus. Jesus died on the cross so that all of our sins can be forgiven. After Jesus rose from the grave, He spent time with Peter. Jesus forgave Peter. You can be forgiven, too. Just tell Jesus you are sorry for the wrong things that you do. When you look at the cross that you made, remember that you can always have a fresh start when you ask for Jesus' forgiveness.

Instruct each child in the following procedures:

- Use clay to make two log-shapes—one about 7x1-inch (18x2.5-cm) and another about 5x1-inch (12.5x2.5-cm).
- Set the shorter log on top of the longer log to make a cross. Press down slightly, then remove the top log and use fingers to apply some water to where the two logs will join. Replace the top log and press together. Turn cross over and add water with fingers to the joint, smoothing clay to join the two logs together (sketch a).
- Pull apart a paper clip slightly to make a hanger for the cross. Insert the flat part of clip into the clay on the back of the cross (sketch b).
- Turn cross over and lay on paper plate. Write name on plate.
- Use fingers and/or plastic fork to make indentations and lines in cross to look like wooden twigs (sketch c).
- Decorate cross by pressing nature items into clay. Dip into water before inserting for a stronger bond. Pine needles may be inserted in the cross to make "rays." Place small pinecones, acorns or seeds in the center of cross (sketch d).
- Allow clay cross to air-dry flat for several days.

Tip: After one or two days of drying, check to see if the nature items are secure in the clay. If they dislodge easily, squeeze craft glue into the indentations and reinsert the items.

Enrichment Idea

- Use the end of a pen or paper clip to carve initials and the date into the back of cross.
- After clay has dried, spray or brush with clear acrylic finish.

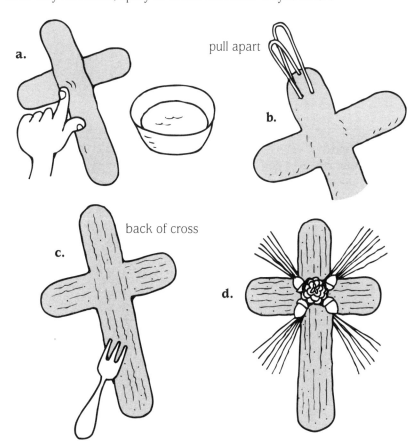

Forest Owl Mobile (25-30 MINUTES)

Materials
- Owl Eyes and Wing Patterns (p. 61)
- brown yarn

For each child—
- 1 brown paper lunch bag

Standard Supplies
- yellow and brown construction paper or card stock
- white paper
- measuring stick
- newspaper
- stapler and staples
- hole punch
- scissors
- craft glue
- transparent tape

Preparation
Copy Wing Patterns onto brown construction paper or card stock—two for each child. Copy Eye Patterns onto white paper—one pair of eyes for each child. Cut yellow construction paper or card stock into 2-inch (5-cm) squares, one for each child. Cut yarn into 1-yard (.9-m) lengths, one for each child.

Conversation
Did you know that owl eyes don't move? Move your eyes from side to side. Now pretend your eyes don't move. How would you see to your right? You would have to turn your head to see. That is why God made owls with a flexible neck. They can turn their head backwards to see what is behind them! God made us able to do special things too, because He loves us so much. What is something special that you can do?

Instruct each child in the following procedures:
- Crumple up newspaper and stuff into lunch bag until bag is filled out, but you can still fold the opening closed.
- Fold down top opening once and have teacher staple bag top closed.
- Punch a hole in the middle of the bag top. Thread length of yarn through the hole. Pull ends even and knot ends together for hanger (sketch a).
- Cut out owl eyes and wings. Fold wings on fold line. Glue eyes and wings onto paper bag. (See sketch b.)
- Fold yellow or gold paper square diagonally to make owl beak. Open owl beak square slightly. Glue two adjoining sides of the beak to the paper bag, so that the beak sticks out slightly (sketch c).

Enrichment Ideas
- Use marker or glitter glue to make a repeated "U" design (see sketch) to create feathers on the owl's chest and wings.
- Children make owlets out of small pinecones. They cut small beaks from yellow construction paper. They glue on beaks and wiggle eyes to the larger end of pinecone. Allow glue to dry. Teacher threads a crewel needle with fishing line and pokes through bottom of bag, brings needle back out the bottom, and removes needle from the fishing line. Children or teachers tie fishing line around pinecone owlets so they hang from the "Mama" owl (see sketch).

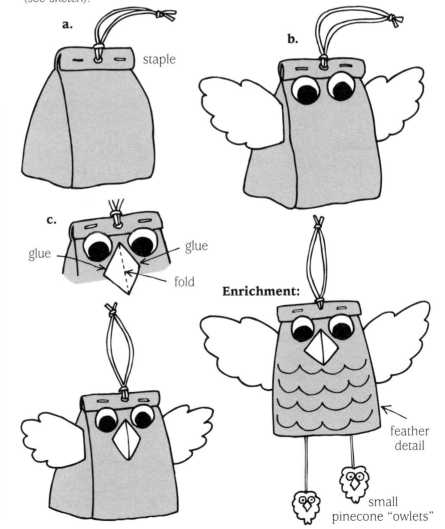

a. staple

b.

c. glue   glue   fold

Enrichment:

feather detail

small pinecone "owlets"

Owl Wing Pattern

(cut two)

Owl Eyes Pattern

"I See Jesus" Sign (25-30 MINUTES)

Materials

- Stick Placement Pattern (p. 63)
- cedar bender board (available at home improvement stores)
- saw
- drill and ⅛-inch (0.3-cm) drill bit
- straight sticks or reeds about ¼ inch (0.6 cm) thick
- plant clippers
- sandpaper
- twine
- carbon paper or art transfer paper

Standard Supplies

- craft glue
- measuring stick
- ballpoint pen

Preparation

Cut bender board into 12- to 14-inch (30.5-cm to 35.5-cm) lengths, one for each child. Drill a hole ½ inch (1.3 cm) from the top edge corner of board (sketch a). Use carbon or transfer paper and Stick Placement Pattern to transfer pattern in the center of each board. Place tracing paper under placement pattern onto board. Trace over each line with a ballpoint pen to transfer pattern to board (sketch b). Repeat for each board. Use plant clippers to cut sticks or reeds into the following sized pieces and numbers for each child: six 2½-inch, three 2-inch, seven 1¼-inch. Cut twine into 30-inch (76-cm) lengths, one for each child.

Conversation

Look at the pattern of the sticks you glued on the wood. Do you see JESUS? In our Bible story, Peter was Jesus' good friend, but it took a while before he really "saw" Jesus and realized Jesus was God's Son. One of the ways we know that Jesus is God's Son is by the things we have learned from the Bible. When you see the sign, remember you know Jesus even though some people haven't learned about Him yet.

Instruct each child in the following procedures:

- Lightly sand the edges of board with sandpaper.
- Thread twine ends through drilled holes. Tie a knot to secure each end to board to make hanger (sketch c).
- Lay board flat on table. Squeeze a line of glue onto the first line of pattern on board.
- Lay a stick that is the same size as the line on top of glue line (sketch d).
- Continue gluing sticks on top of lines, matching stick size to the line size.
- Keep sign flat until glue dries.
- Look at your sign. Can you see "JESUS"?

Simplification Idea

Photocopy Stick Placement Pattern onto colored card stock (two patterns per sheet) and cut apart to make signs. Children glue card-stock sign onto cardboard if desired. Use colored straws instead of sticks from plants. (Note: Use all one color of straws for one sign. Otherwise the optical illusion won't appear.)

Enrichment Ideas

- String a few wooden beads onto twine hanger.
- Spray or brush clear acrylic finish onto completed sign.
- Older children may refer to copies of the Stick Placement Pattern without the need for teacher to trace pattern onto wood.
- Create a border for "I See Jesus" sign with twigs, leaves and other nature items.

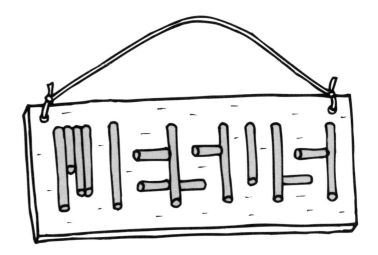

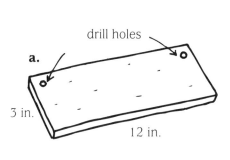

a.

drill holes

3 in.

12 in.

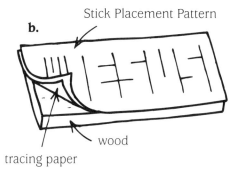

b.

Stick Placement Pattern

wood

tracing paper

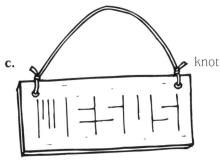

c.

knot

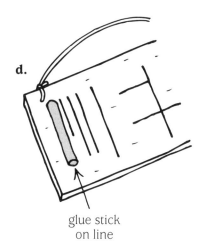

d.

glue stick on line

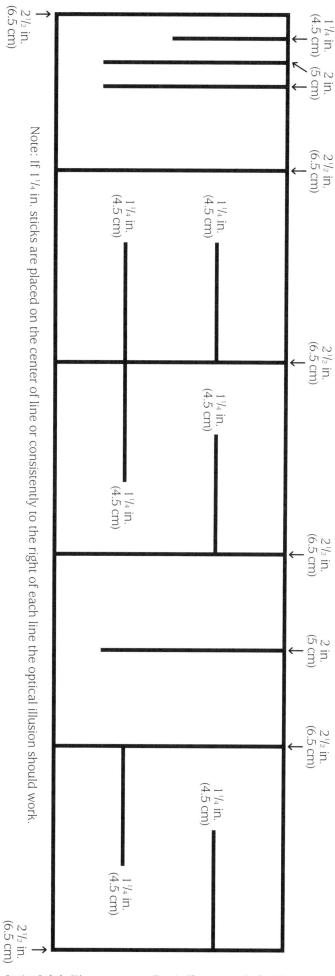

Stick Placement Pattern

Note: If 1¼ in. sticks are placed on the center of line or consistently to the right of each line the optical illusion should work.

2½ in. (6.5 cm)

1¼ in. (4.5 cm)

2 in. (5 cm)

2½ in. (6.5 cm)

1¼ in. (4.5 cm)

1¼ in. (4.5 cm)

2½ in. (6.5 cm)

1¼ in. (4.5 cm)

1¼ in. (4.5 cm)

2½ in. (6.5 cm)

2 in. (5 cm)

2½ in. (6.5 cm)

1¼ in. (4.5 cm)

1¼ in. (4.5 cm)

2½ in. (6.5 cm)

Zip-Line Diorama (25-30 MINUTES)

Materials

- Pine Tree, Mountain and Zip-Line Buddy Patterns (p. 66)
- white, dark green and dark blue or purple card stock
- blue cellophane
- brass or copper wire (20 gauge)
- plastic straws
- variety of small-scale natural items to add to diorama (twigs, bark, pebbles, gravel, moss, etc.)
- red, yellow and/or orange tissue paper
- cotton balls
- wire cutters
- white or glitter crayon
- paper fasteners (brads)

For each child—
- 1 sturdy shoe box without lid

Standard Supplies

- pointed object such as an awl, large paper clip or pointed scissors
- craft glue
- scissors
- blue, green and yellow paper
- tape
- markers or crayons

Preparation

Photocopy Pine Tree Pattern onto dark green card stock, one or more for each child. Photocopy Mountain Pattern onto dark blue or purple card stock, one for each child. Photocopy Zip-Line Buddy Patterns onto white card stock, one or two for each child. Cut additional card stock into 1x5-inch (2.5x12.5-cm) strips (three or four per child). Fold each strip into five equal sections and glue overlapping sections together to make open cube shapes (sketch a). These will be used to stand up cutouts in dioramas. Make one stand for each tree and two for each mountain. Cut green paper in half lengthwise. Cut blue cellophane into 4x10-inch (10x25.5-cm) strips (one or two per child). Cut tissue paper into 4-inch (10-cm) squares (several for each child). Cut wire into 16-inch (40.5-cm) lengths (one per child). Use pointed object to poke two holes in each shoebox where indicated in sketch b. Cut straws into 1/2-inch (1.3-cm) pieces (one per child).

Instruct each child in the following procedures:

- Glue blue paper to cover inside bottom of shoebox. This is the back wall of the diorama.
- Cut green paper to make hills or a mountain range. Glue over the blue paper, at the bottom of back wall (sketch c).
- Cut a circle out of yellow paper for a sun. Cut long rectangles or triangles to make sun's rays. Glue to sky.
- Pull apart cotton balls to make wispy. Glue onto sky for clouds.
- Cut out tree, mountain and Zip-Line Buddy.
- Color top of mountain with white or glitter crayon for snow. Color Zip-Line Buddy.
- Glue a card stock stand to back of mountain at the bottom and another one near the top. Glue a card stock stand to back of tree at the bottom (sketch d). Then squeeze glue on bottoms of stands that will sit on the floor of the box and the part of the stand near the top of the mountain that will rest against the background. Set mountain inside box near the back right side and press glued parts in place. Glue tree near the left side of box towards front.
- Tape small straw piece to back of Zip-Line Buddy. String wire through straw (sketch e).
- Poke each end of wire into holes in box, so wire runs through diorama diagonally. Bend wires to keep in place.
- Poke paper fasteners through holes and open fasteners on inside of box. Twist wire ends around paper fasteners to secure. Teacher may help (sketch f).
- Add details to your mountain scene. Glue sticks in a rock ring to make a campfire. Glue red, orange or yellow tissue paper sticking up between sticks for fire. Cut blue paper into stream shape. Glue to diorama floor. Slightly bunch up blue cellophane and glue on top of blue paper. Glue moss to make plants. Add bark and sticks for logs and glue small rocks and pebbles to the floor (sketch g).
- Now hold your Zip-Line Buddy at the top of the zip-line and let him go . . . ZIP . . . through the mountain air.

Simplification Idea

Eliminate the campfire, stream, and nature items.

Enrichment Ideas

- Children make two zip-lines in diorama with two Zip-Line Buddies. They tape a coin, paper clip or other small object to figures and see which one is faster.
- Children glue dark green triangle shapes to background to make more trees. They create mountain animals or other items out of card stock or construction paper and place in their dioramas.
- Children write the day's verse or key words from the verse on an index card and glue to top of diorama.

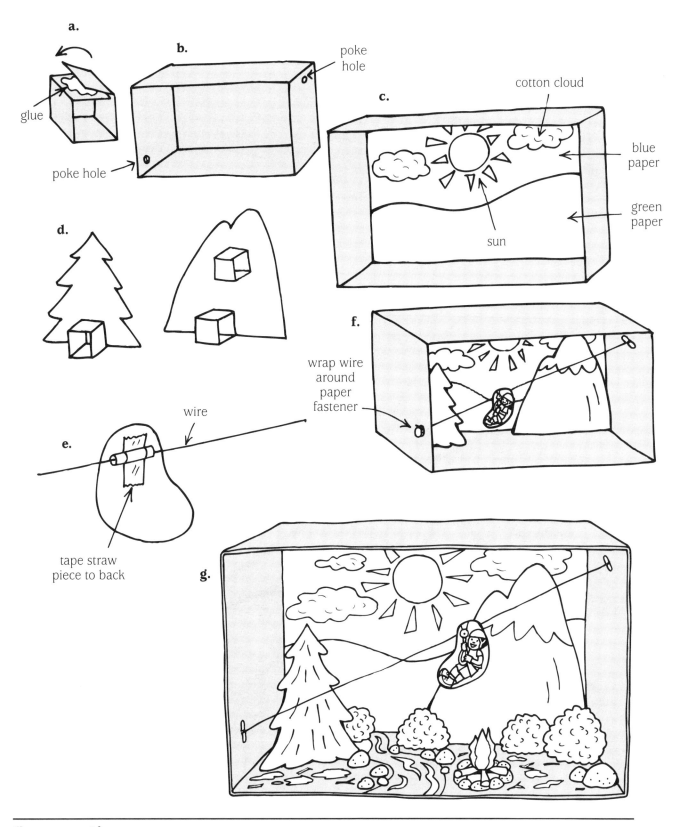

a.

glue

b.

poke hole

poke hole

c.

cotton cloud

blue paper

green paper

sun

d.

e.

wire

tape straw piece to back

f.

wrap wire around paper fastener

g.

Conversation

Have you ever been on a zip-line? How did you feel before you did it? How did you feel after you did it? If you haven't been on one how do you think you might feel? Every day we are in situations that might make us feel a little afraid . . . or a lot afraid. When is a time you remember feeling a little afraid? In our Bible story, Peter became very afraid in the storm, but Jesus was right there to help him and protect him. Jesus is with you, too, when you are afraid. Just remember what the Bible says, *I am the Lord God, who takes hold of your right hand and says to you, Do not fear; I will help you* (Isaiah 41:13).

Mountain Pattern

**Pine Tree
Pattern**

**Zip-Line
Buddy Pattern**

**Zip-Line
Buddy
Pattern**

Mountain Bag (25-30 MINUTES)

Materials

- 9x12-inch (23x30.5-cm) felt sheets in various colors
- adhesive felt sheets and/or small felt nature shapes
- straight pins
- embroidery floss
- wooden beads with large holes
- pony beads
- twine
- sticks 1/4-inch to 1/2-inch thick
- plant clippers

For each child—
- 1 crewel needle

Standard Supplies

- scissors
- measuring stick
- craft glue
- large paper clips

Preparation

Cut felt sheets lengthwise in half to make one 4 1/2 x11-inch (11.5x28-cm) rectangle for each child. Cut sticks into 7- to 8-inch (18- to 20.5-cm) lengths, one for each child. Cut twine into 3-yard (2.7-m) lengths, one for each child. Thread needles with embroidery floss and knot one end.

Conversation

Each of your Mountain Bags looks different, just like you are different from each other. God loves the things that make you different from each other. What is your favorite game to play? What is your favorite food? God loves each one of us. The Bible says, *How great is the love the Father has lavished on us, that we should be called children of God* (1 John 3:1).

Instruct each child in the following procedures:

- Squeeze a line of glue on each side of felt rectangle from the bottom up 4 inches (10 cm) (sketch a).
- Fold up the bottom 4 inches (10 cm) of felt to make bag. Secure glued sides with paper clips (sketch b).
- Place stick above the top of bag pocket. Fold the felt above the stick over the stick to make bag flap. With teacher's help, pin flap over stick to enclose stick between felt (sketch c).
- Use embroidery floss and needle to sew stick inside top flap. Insert needle through the back of bag underneath stick and pull through both thicknesses to the front. Then bring needle to the back again and push under stick, pulling floss through to the front again. Continue to whipstitch the top flap to the stick. With teacher's help, knot at the end (sketch d).
- Decorate the flap and bag front with pieces cut from adhesive felt. Cut pieces to make stripes and shapes and/or use nature shapes. Arrange designs on felt first. Then, when satisfied with design, peel backing off felt shapes and press into place.
- Tie a knot (knot 1) about 8 inches (20.5 cm) from each end of twine.
- String a few beads on one end of twine. Squeeze a little glue on the stick close to the edge of the bag. Wrap the twine around the glued portion a couple of times and then knot (knot 2) to secure (sketch e).
- Repeat with the other end of twine on the other side of bag (sketch f).
- After several hours, remove paper clips from side of bag.
- Use your Mountain Bag to collect nature treasures on outdoor adventures.

Simplification Idea
Teacher sews sides of bags together instead of children gluing them.

Enrichment Idea
With embroidery floss and needles, older children may sew sides together using a simple running stitch.

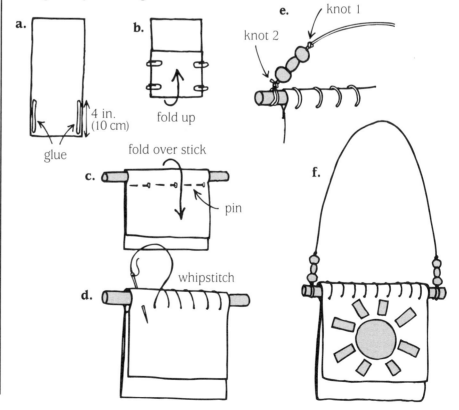

a. / 4 in. (10 cm) / glue
b. fold up
c. fold over stick / pin
d. whipstitch
e. knot 1 / knot 2
f.

Nature Creatures (15 MINUTES)

Materials

- variety of nature items (pinecones, small stones, seed pods, pine needles, leaves, twigs, bark, small feathers, etc.)
- air-drying clay
- wiggle eyes in a variety of sizes

Standard Supplies

- craft glue

Preparation

Set out small lumps of clay and all materials. Make several samples of different creatures.

Conversation

What an interesting bunch of creatures you have made! It's fun to see what you can create using such ordinary objects from nature. God created us, too, but we are far from ordinary. God created us to be able to do good works. The Bible says, *For we are God's workmanship, created in Christ Jesus to do good works, which God prepared in advance for us to do* (Ephesians 2:10). **What are good works? What good works can you do today?**

Instruct each child in the following procedures:

- Choose materials to make your Nature Creature. Pine needles make good whiskers or tails. Leaves and feathers can be used for wings or hair. Small dried berries and seeds are good for noses and ears.
- Use clay and glue to stick items together. First put glue on an object, and then press a small ball of clay on the glue. Squeeze some glue on the other object you want to join to the first object and press into the clay (sketch a).
- Some items may hold together with just glue.
- Add wiggle eyes to your creature.
- Be creative and make a few Nature Creatures.

Simplification Idea

Design one creature for all children to make and collect only those items.

a.

Camp Bugaboo Cabin (25-30 MINUTES)

Materials

- flat brown spray paint
- window screening (available at hardware stores)
- decorative-edged scissors
- thin twigs
- plant clippers

For each child—

- 1 cardboard oatmeal canister with lid

Standard Supplies

- craft knife
- scissors
- newspapers
- construction paper or copier paper in various colors
- markers (including several brown and black)

Preparation

Remove lids from oatmeal canisters and set aside. On each oatmeal canister, draw lines to indicate the cutting lines for a door and two windows with shutters (sketch a). Use a craft knife to cut on lines. Bend back door and shutters to open. Peel off paper labels from canisters. In an outdoor area, spread newspaper and spray canisters with brown paint to cover. Cut twigs into 1/2- to 1-inch (1.3- to 2.5-cm) pieces—at least five for each child. Cut some of the colored paper into 1/2-inch (1.3-cm) strips. Cut window screening into 5 1/2x13-inch (14x33-cm) rectangles, one for each child.

Conversation

What kind of bugs do you think you will find to put in your Bug Cabin? What do you think your bugs would like to eat? Make sure you put some leaves, twigs and grass in your bug's new home. You can use a small bottle cap to hold water for your bugs to drink. It's your job to make sure your bugs have everything they need while you are watching them. We are fortunate to have parents and adults who look out for us. Jesus helps and protects us by giving us people in our lives to take care of us every day.

Instruct each child in the following procedures:

- Use black or brown markers to draw wooden boards on each shutter and the door (sketch b).
- Use decorative-edged scissors to cut one edge of paper strips.
- Cut strips into lengths to fit around each window and door. Glue strips onto canister around windows and doors (sketch c).
- Make a sign out of colored paper for your cabin and glue it above the door.
- Roll up window screen and insert inside the canister. Smooth against the walls. Glue along the overlapping edge of screen inside (sketch d).
- Put lid on oatmeal canister.
- Glue small twigs to the shutter doors and large door for door handles. Add twigs to outline your sign, if desired (sketch e).

Simplification Idea

Eliminate cutting paper strips with fancy scissors and gluing on twig decorations.

Enrichment Ideas

- Children paint oatmeal canister with tempera paints and allow to dry overnight. Finish the following day.
- Children add further details to cabin with markers, colored paper, and/or stickers such as grass, plants, flowers and bugs.

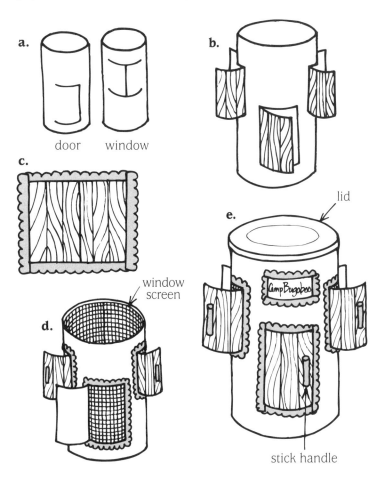

a.   door   window

b.

c.

d.   window screen

e.   lid

Camp Bugaboo

stick handle

Walking on Water Window (25-30 MINUTES)

Materials

- Jesus, Peter and Boat Patterns (p. 72)
- craft foam in blue, white and brown
- cotton balls
- muslin fabric
- tongue depressors

For each child—
- two large blue disposable plastic plates

Standard Supplies

- white card stock
- ruler
- scissors
- black markers
- crayons
- craft glue and/or craft glue dots
- low temp glue gun and glue sticks

Preparation

Photocopy Jesus and Peter Patterns onto card stock, one each for each child. Trace Boat Pattern onto brown craft foam, one boat for each child. Cut muslin into 2-inch (5-cm) squares, one for each child. Cut out the center of plastic plates as shown in sketch a, one for each child. Cut blue craft foam into 2x8-inch (5x20.5-cm) strips, two for each child.

Conversation

You can use your stick puppets to act out today's Bible story. In our Bible story, Peter started out walking on the water, but grew afraid when he saw the waves and wind around him. Then he started to sink and Jesus helped him. When are some times kids might be afraid? When we are afraid, we can remember that Jesus is helping and protecting us in every situation. We can talk to him whenever we are afraid. The Bible says, *I am the Lord, your God, who takes hold of your right hand and says to you, Do not fear; I will help you* (Isaiah 41:13).

Instruct each child in the following procedures:

- Color Jesus and Peter patterns with crayons. Cut out.
- Cut foam along edge of cutout patterns.
- Attach depressor with glue by sandwiching it between each cutout and craft foam piece. Set aside to dry (sketch b).
- Cut waves on one long edge of each blue craft foam strip.
- Glue one wave strip to the cut edge of plastic plate window on the inside of plate. Trim ends to fit if necessary (sketch c).
- Lay the window plate on top of the whole plate with the insides of plates facing each other. Position the second blue wave strip on the second plate so that it is slightly higher than the wave strip on the window plate (sketch d). Remove the window plate and glue the second wave strip to the whole plate, trimming edges to fit.
- Cut out boat from brown craft foam. Cut a thin brown strip for the boat mast.
- Lift up the wave strip on the whole plate and glue the boat slightly under it. Glue on the mast.
- Glue muslin square over the mast for the boat's sail (sketch e).
- Gently stretch cotton ball clouds and glue next to boat in the sky.
- Teacher applies hot glue around the plate edge, leaving the bottom 7 inches (18 cm) of the plate unglued (sketch f). Quickly place the window plate on top of the whole plate. Teacher presses edges to seal.
- After glue has set, insert Jesus and Peter figures through the window and then slide tongue depressor handles through the unglued edges of plates (sketch g).
- Move Jesus and Peter through the water in the window.

Simplification Ideas

- Eliminate using craft foam by using colored card stock.
- Eliminate making the clouds and the boat.
- Use paper plates and white glue instead of plastic plates and a glue gun.

Enrichment Idea

Use glitter glue pens to add more wave designs to craft foam and plastic plates. Add lightning in the sky with glitter glue. Allow glitter glue to dry thoroughly before inserting figures.

© 2009 Gospel Light. Permission to photocopy granted to original purchaser only. *Camp Creations Crafts for Kids*

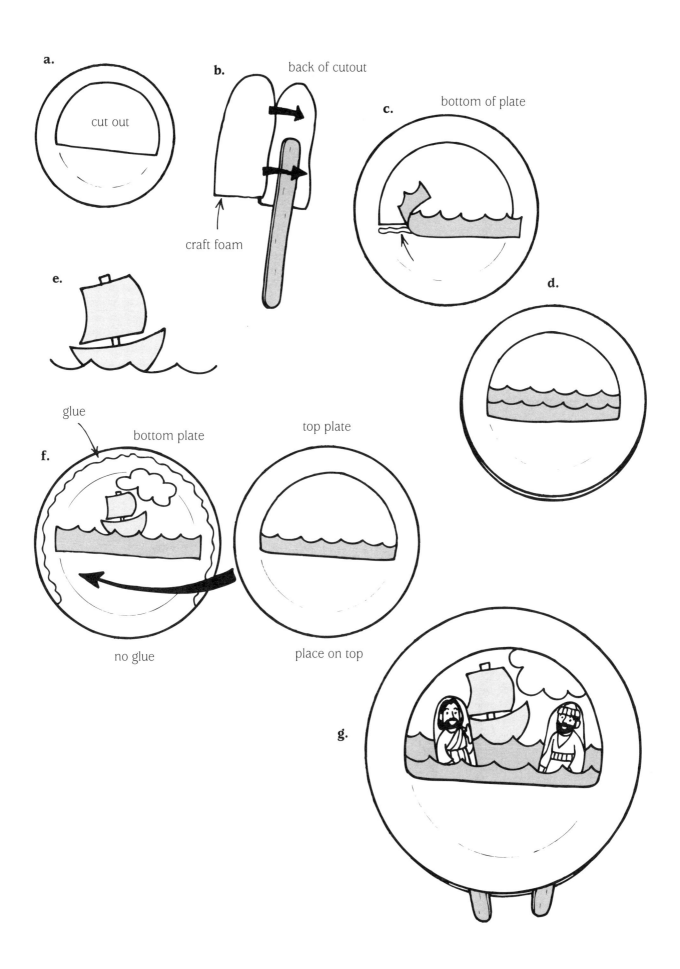

a. cut out

b. back of cutout

craft foam

c. bottom of plate

d.

e.

f. glue
bottom plate
no glue

top plate
place on top

g.

Jesus Pattern

Peter Pattern

Boat Pattern

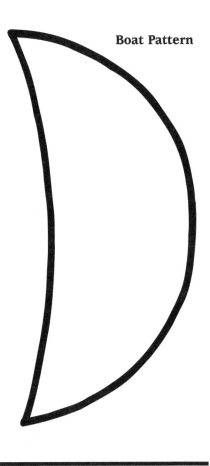

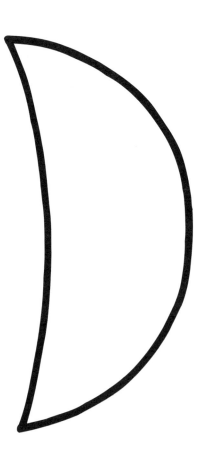

• Younger Elementary • Grades 1-3 •

Peter's Catch Bookmark (20-25 MINUTES)

Materials

- plastic lacing in various colors
- plastic beads

For each child—

- 6 fish-shaped beads (wooden, plastic or glass)

Standard Supplies

- measuring stick
- scissors
- shallow containers
- masking tape

Preparation

Cut plastic lacing into 24-inch (61-cm) lengths, three for each child. Place beads in shallow containers.

Conversation

Peter worked as a fisherman. One day, when he was fishing, Jesus asked Peter to follow Him. That meant he wanted Peter to travel with Him, get to know Him and learn from Him about God. How do you think Peter felt when Jesus wanted him to be His friend? Today, Jesus calls all of us His friends. He loves us and accepts us, too. When you see your bookmark, you can remember Peter the fisherman and remember that Jesus loves you!

Instruct each child in the following procedures:

- Hold three strands of plastic lacing together and tie in an overhand knot about 5 inches (12.5 cm) from the ends. Pull lacing to secure (sketch a).
- On each lacing above the knot, string four to five plastic beads. Then string on a fish bead. Tie a knot in the end of each lacing so beads do not slip off (sketch b).
- Braid the lacing strands above the knot. Stop braiding about 4 inches (10 cm) from the end of strands (sketch c). Use masking tape to attach bookmark to the table while braiding.
- With teacher's help, hold strands together and tie in an overhand knot near the end of braiding.
- On each lacing strand above knot, string only two beads and then a fish bead. Knot near the fish bead to secure (sketch d).
- Use your bookmark by placing the braid down the page, with the fish ends sticking out of each end of book.

Simplification Ideas

- Instead of braiding, children knot the three strands together every 2 to 3 inches (5 to 7.5 cm).

Enrichment Idea

Children make one to keep and one to give to a friend. Children decorate envelopes to put a bookmark in as a gift.

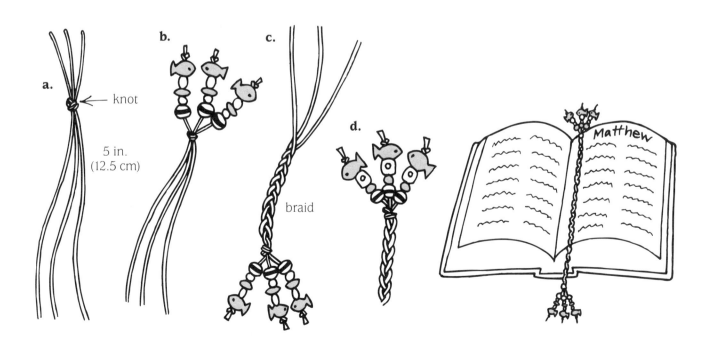

Camp Canoe Frame (25-30 MINUTES)

Materials
- Canoe Pattern (p. 75)
- craft foam in a variety of colors
- small adhesive-back craft foam shapes
- yarn
- tongue depressors
- craft sticks

Standard Supplies
- hole punch
- card stock
- scissors
- craft glue
- low-temp glue gun and glue sticks
- measuring stick
- masking tape
- pencils
- fine-tip permanent markers

Preparation
Trace Canoe Pattern onto craft foam and cut out, one for each child. Punch four holes in one side of each canoe (see sketch d). Fold canoe so the sides meet. Use pencil to make corresponding marks in the matching side. Then use the marks as a guide to punch holes that will line up with the first holes. Repeat procedure for the opposite end of canoe. Cut yarn into 2-foot (61-cm) lengths, two for each child. Cut card stock into 4$\frac{1}{2}$x5$\frac{1}{2}$-inch (11.5x14 cm) rectangles, one for each child.

Conversation
Have you ever been in a canoe or kayak on a lake? When the wind blew, what happened to your canoe? In our Bible story, Peter and his friends were in a boat on a lake when a big windstorm came up. They were so afraid; they thought that they would sink. When you are afraid, or when you look at your canoe photo frame you can remember that Jesus can help and protect you.

Instruct each child in the following procedures:
- Glue a craft stick to each short side of card-stock rectangle.
- Glue a tongue depressor across the bottom edge of card stock, with the ends on top of craft sticks (sketch a).
- If desired, use a pencil to write "SonRock Kids Camp 2009" across another tongue depressor. Then trace over the pencil with a fine-tip permanent marker.
- Squeeze glue only on the top ends of craft sticks and place the second tongue depressor across the top of frame so that a photo can slide through between the tongue depressor and the card stock back (sketch b). Set frame aside to dry.
- Fold craft foam canoe so that holes line up. Thread one length of yarn through the two bottom holes (sketch c). Pull the yarn ends even. With teacher's help, wrap a small piece of masking tape around the ends to make a "needle."
- Bring the "needle" and yarn through the back of the next three holes to sew the canoe side together. Continue coming through the back of holes, making a whipstitch. At the top hole bring needle and yarn through the hole twice. Repeat process using second length of yarn on the other side of canoe (sketch d).
- Tie the two ends of yarn together at the top to make a hanger. Trim the tape from the yarn ends.
- Decorate the front of canoe with adhesive craft foam shapes.
- With teacher's help, use glue gun to glue the back of the frame inside the canoe (sketch e).
- Tape the yarn hanger to the back of frame, so it lies behind the frame (sketch f).
- After glue has dried, slide a 3x5-inch (7.5x12.5-cm) photo through the top of frame and hang Canoe Frame on the wall.

Simplification Idea
Use only one-half of Canoe Pattern to make a flat canoe shape. This eliminates the lacing. Glue the top of canoe to the bottom of frame.

Enrichment Ideas
- Take a photo of each child at VBS. Print as 3x5-inch (7.5x12.5-cm) photos and insert into frames.
- Use colored markers or three-dimensional paint to decorate the craft sticks and tongue depressors.

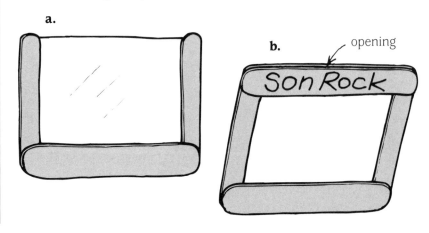

a.

b.

opening

SonRock

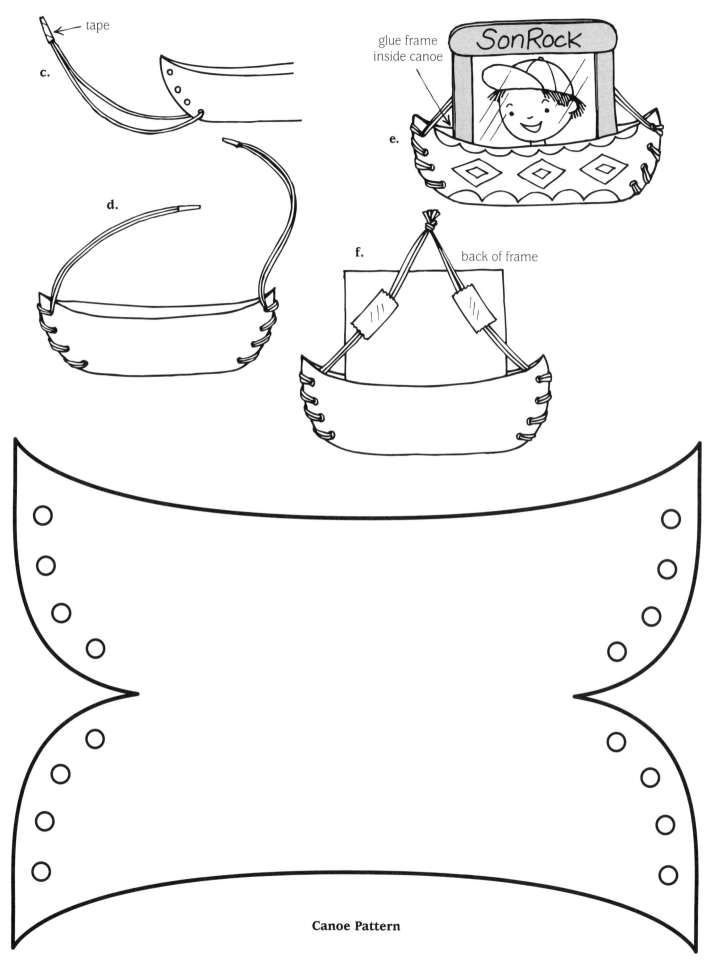

tape

c.

glue frame
inside canoe

SonRock

e.

d.

f.   back of frame

Canoe Pattern

Camp Pennant (15-20 MINUTES)

Materials

- large craft foam sheets in various colors
- small craft foam shapes
- three-dimensional paints in squeeze bottles
- plastic beads
- ¼-inch (0.6-cm) wooden dowels
- hand saw

Standard Supplies

- permanent markers
- scissors
- ruler
- hole punch
- masking tape

Preparation

Cut craft foam sheets into pennant triangles with two sides 12 inches (30.5 cm) and one side 9 inches (23 cm), one for each child (sketch a). Cut dowels into 18-inch (45.5-cm) lengths, one for each child.

Conversation

What have you enjoyed the most at SonRock Kids Camp so far? Your pennant can remind you of the great time you had with all your camp friends. It can also remind you about all the things you learned about Jesus and how He cares for you. What are some things you learned about Jesus? (He accepts us; He protects us; He saves us; He forgives us; He gives us strength to do good.)

Instruct each child in the following procedures:

- Use pencil to write your name; SonRock Kids Camp 2009; the name of your class or a Daily Truth. Then trace over letters with marker.
- Punch three evenly spaced holes on the short side of pennant.
- Thread dowel through holes for pennant stick.
- Secure pennant to dowel with masking tape.
- Decorate pennant by gluing on foam shapes and beads.
- Use three-dimensional paints to accent. Trace over the first letter of words. Use paints to make dots and squiggle designs or to add details to foam shapes.
- Allow to dry flat.

Simplification Idea

Make pennants out of brightly colored card stock or poster board and decorate with glitter glue, markers, stickers and sequins.

Enrichment Ideas

- Glue on foam letters to make words on pennants.
- Decorate with small pom-poms as well as other supplies.

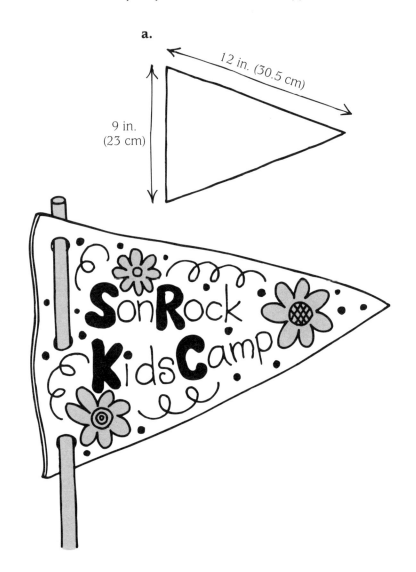

a.

12 in. (30.5 cm)

9 in. (23 cm)

Crafts for Older Elementary

Planning craft projects for older children can be fun. These children have well-developed skills to complete more complicated projects and they love the chance to use those skills. However, preteens also have well-developed preferences about what they want to do. Sometimes a challenging project may not appeal to these young sophisticates, while a project that seems too juvenile to the adult will click with the kids!

We think you'll find projects in this section to satisfy the varied tastes of older elementary children. But a sense of humor and these tips will surely help: Filter craft ideas through a panel of experts—two or three fifth graders! If they like something, chances are the rest of the group will, too. Also, the better you get to know your children, the better your batting average will be. Remember, kids enjoy adapting crafts to express their own personalities—so put out a few extra supplies such as wiggle eyes, glitter glue, and fabric or paper scraps. You just might be surprised at what they dream up!

Backpack It Up (Two-Day Craft/45-60 minutes total time)

Materials

- tall kitchen garbage bags
- duct tape in a variety of colors
- decorative materials (stickers, paint pens, etc.)

For each child—

- 2-inch (5-cm) piece of adhesive-backed Velcro

Standard Supplies

- scissors
- measuring stick
- permanent markers

Conversation

Backpacks are handy things to have. When you go on a hike, you can bring snacks and other things you might need for protection like a jacket in case it gets cold, or sunblock for sunny days. What are some other things you could put in your backpack? Allow children to share their ideas. Whether or not you have your backpack, wherever you go, you can know that Jesus will help and protect you. In Isaiah 41:13 the Bible tells us "I am the LORD, your God, who takes hold of your right hand and says to you, Do not fear; I will help you." We can ask Jesus for His protection in EVERY situation! Encourage children to identify situations in which they can rely on Jesus' power and protection.

Day One Preparation
Instruct each child in the following procedures:

- Cut top off kitchen garbage bag (if there are handles). Cut bottom off and cut one side open. Spread bag on table. Use measuring stick to measure a 12x30-inch (30.5x76-cm) rectangle (sketch a).
- Apply strips of duct tape across the rectangle. Alternate colors or use all the same color if you like (sketch b). Fold top and bottom piece of tape over plastic bag to finish edge of duct tape material. Trim to size of rectangle.

Tip: Lick fingers to keep duct tape from sticking to them as you work.

- Fold bag in half, with duct tape sides together, to make a 12x15-inch (30.5x38-cm) rectangle.
- Cut 20-inch (51-cm) lengths of duct tape. Fold in half lengthwise (sticky sides together) to make straps. Trim.
- Place straps inside of bag make the end of the straps come out of the sides. Use small pieces of tape to attach end of straps to sides, 3 inches (7.5 cm) from the bottom (sketch c).
- With backpack inside out, tape along each side, closing the side seams; trim ends (sketch d). Write name on the inside of bag.

Day Two
Instruct each child in the following procedures:

- Place straps towards the back of bag. Use a small piece of tape to attach straps to top edge, 3 inches (7.5 cm) from sides. Secure straps by placing duct tape across the width of the inside of front and back of backpack (sketch e).
- Attach Velcro to inside of center top edge.
- Turn bag right side out. Push out sides and bottom corners of bag.
- Tape over side seams; trim ends (sketch f).
- Decorate as time allows. Use markers or paint pens to write memory verses or the Daily Truth statements on backpacks. Place stickers (a variety of theme-related stickers are available from Gospel Light), on backpacks as desired.

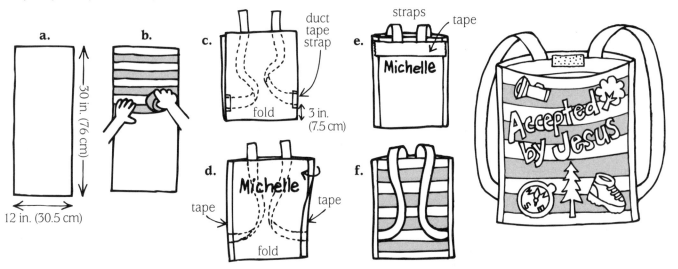

Basket Weaving (15-20 minutes)

Materials
- variety of chenille wires
- mugs or other drinking cups

Optional—
- beads (wooden beads available from Gospel Light)

Standard Supplies
- scissors

Conversation

There are lots of things you can put in your basket. What will you put in your basket, Jen? Some people put gifts in baskets instead of wrapping them.

The best gift anyone can get doesn't come in a basket. Because Jesus is the Savior, He gives us salvation and eternal life. All we have to do is accept His wonderful gift and we can become members of God's family and live with Jesus forever!

Instruct each child in the following procedures:

- Select five chenille wires. Bend wires in half. Use end of one wire to wrap wires together at bend (sketch a).
- Keeping wire end used to wrap other wires separate, spread wires apart an equal distance. Turn mug upside down on table. Place wires over end of mug and press edges down over sides (sketch b). Remove mug when satisfied with shape.
- Begin weaving with end of chenille wire used to wrap wires together. Continue weaving over and under other wires until you reach end of wire. Attach a new wire and continue weaving (sketch c). (Optional: Occasionally thread a bead on chenille wire as you weave.) Continue weaving to desired height.
- Finish basket by bending over ends of wires that are sticking up and threading through previous weaving (sketch d). (Optional: Children may add handles by twisting two wires together and attaching to sides of basket.)

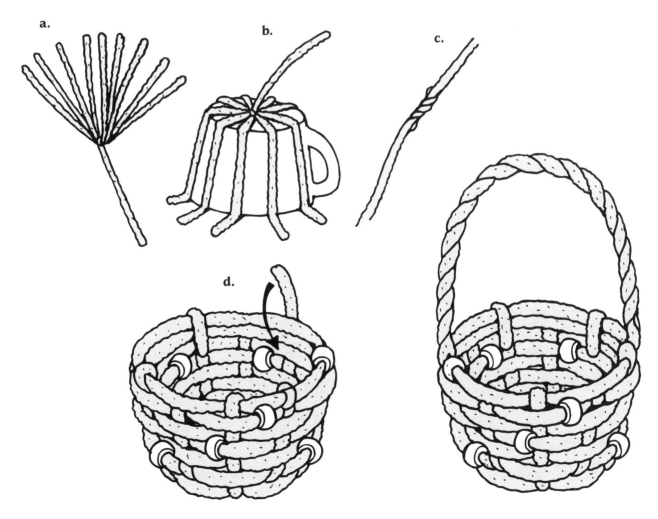

a.

b.

c.

d.

Hiker's Cross and Belt-Loop Lanyard

(25-30 minutes)

Materials

- plastic lacing in a variety of colors

For each child—

- flexible party favor bracelet about 3 inches (7.5 cm) in diameter (available at party-supply stores)
- 17 glow-in-the-dark pony beads
- lanyard clip
- split-ring key ring

Standard Supplies

- measuring stick
- scissors

Preparation

For each child, cut one 16-inch (40.5-cm), one 12-inch (30.5-cm) and two 24-inch (61-cm) pieces of plastic lacing.

Conversation

There are lots of things you can put on your lanyard: keys, a compass or a whistle are some of your options. When might you need a lanyard with a whistle on it? (To signal if lost. To get help if someone is hurt.) A compass and a whistle are both things than can help protect you from danger. The cross can remind you that Jesus will help and protect you because Jesus is with you all the time!

Instruct each child in the following procedures:

- Fold 16-inch (40.5-cm) piece of lacing in half and tie a knot about $1/2$ inch (1.3 cm) below fold (sketch a).
- Below the knot, place one side of bracelet between lacing strands. String four beads onto both lacing strands, sliding them up to just below knot and bracelet (sketch b).
- Place the 12-inch (30.5-cm) piece of lacing between the two lacing strands and then thread seven more beads onto the lacing strands (sketch b).
- Separate strands of lacing below the beads and place the opposite side of bracelet between them. Tie a tight overhand knot just below the bracelet (sketch b). Trim ends of lacing.
- To make the crossbar, string three beads on each end of the short piece of lacing. Wrap lacing strands around sides of bracelet and thread back through the beads (sketch c).
- Tie ends of crossbar lacing in a knot at center back of cross (sketch d). Thread ends back through beads and trim excess lacing to finish Hiker's Cross.
- Thread two 24-inch (61-cm) pieces of lacing through lanyard hook. Fold lacing in half to find the centers. Place hook at center of both pieces of lacing. Separate strands to form an X (sketch e).
- Use square stitch to form lanyard. Take one length and form a loop over the hook. Take the other end of the same lacing and form a second loop over the hook (sketch f).
- Thread one end of other lacing over the loop nearest it, and under the other loop. Thread the other end of lacing over the second loop and under the first loop (sketch g).
- Pull all four lacing ends to tighten stitch (sketch f).
- Continue with square stitch until you have about 4 inches (10 cm). (Optional: Thread a couple of beads onto lacings.) Slip a split-ring over ends of lacings and tie an overhand knot. Trim ends. Slide Hiker's Cross onto split ring.

Simplification Idea

Instead of making Belt-Loop Lanyard, attach Hiker's Cross to a long length of lacing to wear as a necklace.

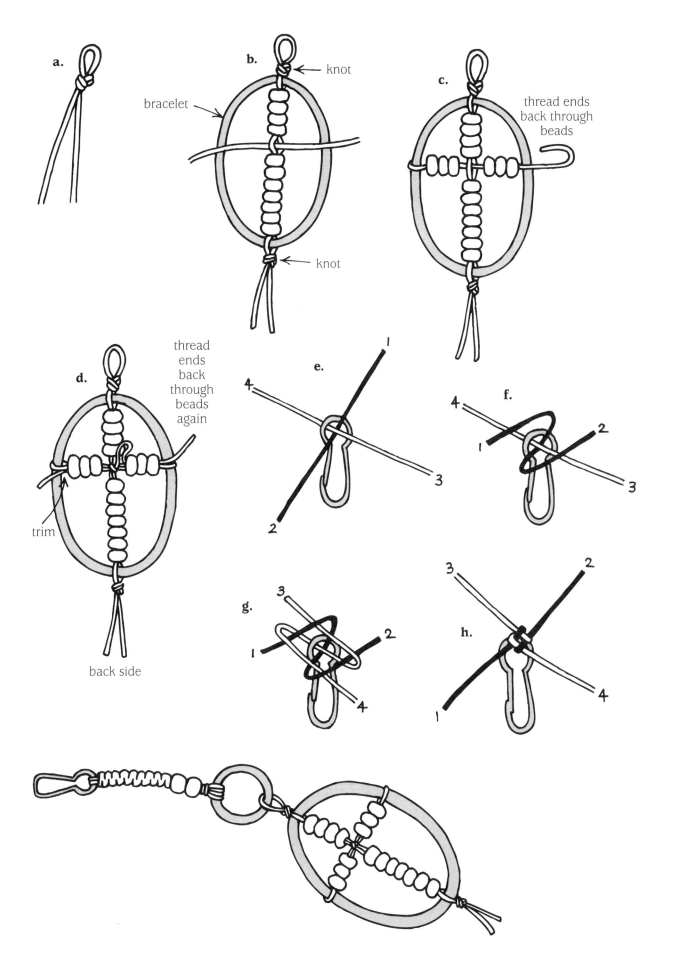

a.

b.
knot
bracelet
knot

c.
thread ends
back through
beads

d.
thread
ends
back
through
beads
again
trim
back side

e.
4
1
2
3

f.
4
1
2
3

g.
3
1
2
4

h.
3
1
2
4

Camp Journal (Two-Day Craft/45-60 minutes total time)

Materials
- cardboard
- decorative papers (scrapbook papers, handmade papers, etc.)
- colored card stock
- water
- scrap paper
- twine or leather lacing
- leather scraps
- decorative materials (stickers, wood beads, feathers, etc.)

For every 2 or 3 children—
- small bowl

For each child—
- sponge brush
- filler paper (several copies of "Journal Page" p. 84; and/or several sheets of 6x9-inch [15x23-cm] paper.)

Standard Supplies
- newspaper
- white glue or craft glue
- scissors
- hole punches

Conversation
Many people start new journals every year on their birthdays or at New Year's. They like to start the year with a fresh new start! Your journal is blank—you can fill it with whatever you like. We become like a blank book when we receive Jesus' forgiveness, because Jesus gives us a fresh start. You can use the fresh start Jesus gives you to fill your life with good things by doing right actions. In Psalm 86:5 our Bible says, "You are forgiving and good, O Lord, abounding in love to all who call to you." We can call to Jesus for forgiveness when we do wrong. Because He loves us, Jesus forgives us!

Day One Preparation
Cover tables with newspapers. For each child, cut cardboard into three pieces with the following dimensions (sketch a): 1x9 inches (2.5x23 cm), 5$\frac{1}{2}$x9 inches (14x23 cm) and 6$\frac{1}{2}$x9 inches (16.5x23 cm). This will make the spine, front cover and back cover, respectively.

In each bowl, mix equal parts glue and water and stir with sponge brush to a milky consistency.

Budget Tip: Save money on sponge brushes. Cut inexpensive kitchen sponges into 2-inch (5-cm) squares. Clip to a clothespin to make your own sponge brushes.

Instruct each child in the following procedures:
- Cut or tear one or more pieces of paper to cover cardboard, making sure the paper is larger than the cardboard piece. Use sponge brush to apply glue mixture to cardboard pieces, one piece at a time. Smooth on cardboard (sketch b). Repeat for all three cardboard pieces.
- Flip cardboard over and trim corners from paper (sketch c).
- Brush glue on edges of back. Fold ends of paper over back of cardboard (sketch d). Continue for all three pieces of cardboard.
- Children write names on each piece of cardboard and set aside to dry.

Day Two Preparation
Cut card stock into 5x8$\frac{1}{2}$-inch (12.5x21.5-cm) and 6x8$\frac{1}{2}$-inch (15x21.5-cm) pieces, cutting one of each for each child. Cut twine or leather lacing into pieces approximately 30 inches (76 cm) long.

Instruct each child in the following procedures:
- Glue card-stock pieces to backs of covers, using the larger card-stock piece on the back cover and the smaller card-stock piece on the front cover (sketch e). (You do not need to glue anything to the back of the spine.)
- In filler pages, punch three holes spaced equally apart along left edge (sketch f).
- Place a filler page on inside of back cover. Mark an X where each hole lines up. Use hole punch to punch holes (sketch g). Repeat on spine.
- Sandwich back cover, filler paper and spine. Starting with top hole, children thread lacing through holes and tie in front.
- Cut leather scraps to use as hinges. Place front cover next to spine and glue on hinges (sketch h). Use decorative materials to decorate journals. Don't forget to decorate the inside covers!

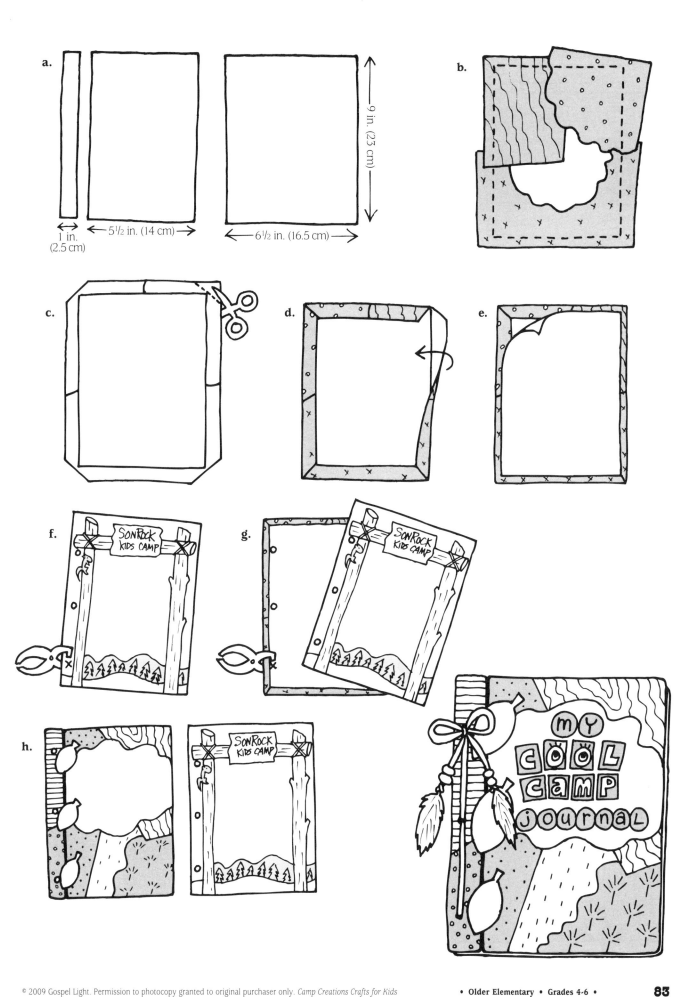

a.

1 in.
(2.5 cm)

5½ in. (14 cm)

6½ in. (16.5 cm)

9 in. (23 cm)

b.

c.

d.

e.

f.

SonRock
Kids Camp

g.

SonRock
Kids Camp

h.

SonRock
Kids Camp

My
Cool
Camp
Journal

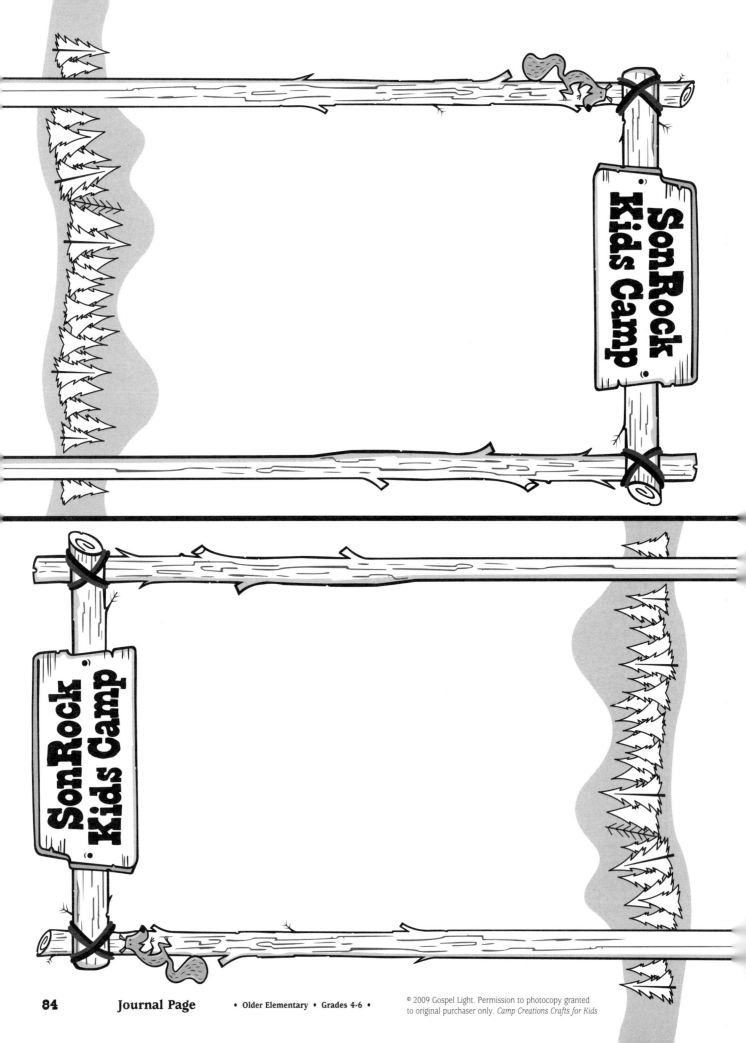

SonRock
Kids Camp

SonRock
Kids Camp

Flowering Tiles (20-30 minutes)

Materials

- variety of decorative paper (handmade papers, card stock, scrapbook papers, etc.)
- assortment of pressed flowers and leaves
- clear acrylic spray

Optional—
- feathers
- stickers (SonRock Assortment Stickers available from Gospel Light)

For every 2 or 3 children—
- small bowl

For each child—
- sponge brush
- Two 3-inch (7.5-cm) solid-colored ceramic tiles
- 2 picture hangers

Standard Supplies

- newspaper
- craft glue
- water
- craft cement
- ballpoint pens

Preparation

Cover tables with newspaper. In each bowl, mix equal parts glue and water and stir with sponge brush to a milky consistency. Use craft cement to secure a picture hanger to the back of each tile.

Conversation

These flowery tiles make beautiful decorations. But more than that, they remind us about who we are in Jesus. Which verse did you put on your tile? What does that verse tell us about who we are in Jesus? What is today's verse? Lead child to repeat the words of Romans 10:9. This verse tells us that we can be saved by Jesus! When we are saved by Jesus we become members of God's family and will live with Jesus now and forever!

Instruct each child in the following procedures:

- Tear a piece of decorative paper to fit onto tile. Use a ballpoint pen to write a VBS memory verse on paper.
- Brush tile with glue mixture. Place paper on tile and brush lightly with glue (sketch a).
- Brush tile with glue mixture. Select flowers and leaves and place on tile. Use brush handle to tap down on each petal and leaf. (Try not to touch the flowers with your fingers. Any glue on your fingers will cause the flowers to stick to them and tear. See sketch b.)
- (Optional: Children place feathers on tiles and/or stickers on tiles.)
- Once flowers are positioned the way you like, lightly dab glue mixture over entire front of tile. Set tiles aside to dry.
- When dry, craft leader and/or helpers spray with clear acrylic spray.

Budget Tip: Instead of glazing tiles with clear acrylic spray, use acrylic floor polish. Brush tiles lightly to cover. When dry, brush with a second coat.

Enrichment Idea

Check out books on wildflowers from the library. Children identify flowers they used for their projects.

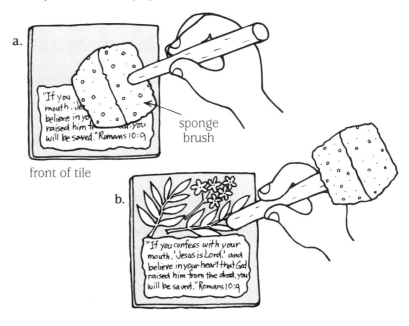

front of tile

Leaf Plate (20-30 minutes)

Materials

- variety of real or plastic leaves, 5 to 6 inches (12.5 to 15 cm) in size
- play dough rollers, brayers, or 6- to 8-inch (15- to 20.5-cm) pieces of PVC pipe
- paper bowls or other oven-safe bowls

For every 2 children—
- 2-oz. (60-ml) package of polymer clay (provide a variety of colors)

For each child—
- plastic knife
- resealable plastic bag, snack or sandwich size
- sheet of waxed paper

Standard Supplies

- water

Preparation

Open polymer clay packages and use plastic knife to cut each block in half, creating 1-oz. (30-ml) pieces. Place each piece of clay in a separate resealable plastic bag and seal. Place water in bowls and place on tables where children will be working.

Conversation

Our leaf plates make great decorations for our rooms. We can put coins or jewelry in our leaf plates. But more than that, our leaf plates can remind us of today's Daily Truth. What is today's Daily Truth? (Living for Jesus.) **Just like God created the leaves on the trees, God created us. In Ephesians 2:10 our Bibles tell us, "For we are God's workmanship, created in Christ Jesus to do good works, which God prepared in advance for us to do." When we see our leaf, we can remember that God created us to do good works and that Jesus will give us the strength we need to do the good things He has planned for us.**

Instruct each child in the following procedures:

- Select a leaf and a piece of polymer clay. Remove it from bag and play with the clay, kneading, folding and rolling it for a couple of minutes. This conditions the clay and makes it easier to work with. The clay is conditioned when you can roll it into a log, fold it and the clay doesn't break (sketch a).

- Form clay into a ball and then press ball flat, using your hands to flatten clay. Place clay on sheet of waxed paper. Use a play dough roller, brayer or piece of PVC pipe to smooth and roll out the clay so that it is bigger than the leaf you selected.

- Sprinkle some water on clay. Sprinkle some water on the underside of your leaf. Place leaf FACEUP on clay and use play dough roller, brayer or piece of PVC pipe to roll leaf into clay (sketch b).

- Use plastic knife to cut around the leaf (sketch c). Tear extra clay away from cut shape. Place extra clay in resealable plastic bag and seal.

- Carefully lift leaf off of clay, and then gently lift clay off of waxed paper and flip clay over. Use tip of knife to gently scratch your initials on the backside of the leaf. Be sure not to press hard enough to go through your leaf (sketch d)!

- After class, leader flips paper bowls or other oven-safe bowls upside down and drapes leaves facedown on bowls. (Optional: For rounder shapes, drape leaves over light bulbs or cardboard tubes.) Then leader places bowls in oven and bakes according to polymer clay manufacturer's instructions. (Usually 265° F or 275° F for about 15-30 minutes. Paper bowls do not burn at this low temperature.) You can bake in either a regular oven or toaster oven. Allow leaves to cool before taking off of bowls.

Tip: Leaves can cool inside the oven. Just turn off the oven and let the leaves sit until cool. Once they have cooled, they will retain their draped shape. When it comes to baking polymer clay, you can bake LONGER than the time specified, but NEVER bake at a higher temperature than the manufacturer recommends.

Alternate Ideas

- Children mix herbs or other dried plant materials into clay before rolling out.

- Instead of pressing leaves into clay and cutting out, children use leaf-shaped cookie cutters to cut out leaf shapes. Children then etch veins into clay using tip of plastic knives or toothpicks.

a.

b.

c.

d.

Embossed Metal Magnet (20-30 minutes)

Materials

- Animal Patterns (p. 89)
- thin sheets of copper, brass and/or aluminum (available from craft stores and home improvement stores)
- magnets

For each child—
- crochet hook, stylus or other rounded instrument such as a ballpoint pen

Standard Supplies

- ruler
- scissors
- masking tape
- newspaper and/or magazines
- craft sticks
- craft glue

Preparation

Cut copper, brass and/or aluminum sheets into 6x6-inch (15x15-cm) pieces. Photocopy Animal Patterns, enlarging so that image will fit metal pieces well. Make several copies of each pattern and cut apart.

Conversation

Animals all have different forms of protection. Skunks have a smelly oil they can spray to discourage predators. Porcupines have quills. Other animals have camouflage or are colored to blend into their environment. Some have strong arms, teeth and claws that discourage attackers.

But we have the best form of protection—Jesus! In Isaiah 41:13, our Bible tells us "I am the Lord, your God, who takes hold of your right hand and says to you, Do not fear; I will help you." I'm glad to know that in any situation, I can be helped and protected by Jesus.

Instruct each child in the following procedures:

- Choose an animal pattern and tape to the back of a piece of metal sheet (sketch a).
- Place metal-sheet piece on a stack of newspapers or a magazine (sketch a).
- Using crochet hook, stylus or other instrument, press hard and trace the lines of the pattern (sketch a).
- Remove pattern and turn metal-sheet piece over. Use craft stick to press down and rub against metal between traced lines. This will enhance the embossed lines.
- Use scissors to cut around animal about ⅛-inch (.3-cm) beyond outline. Or turn edges toward back and use craft stick to press down on fold (sketch b).
- Glue magnet to back of embossed design.

Enrichment Idea
Instead of using patterns, children draw their own designs to emboss on metal sheets.

Budget Tip: Collect promotional magnets, the magnetic sheets with advertisements printed on one side. Cut the sheets into smaller pieces to glue on the backs of the finished embossed-metal crafts.

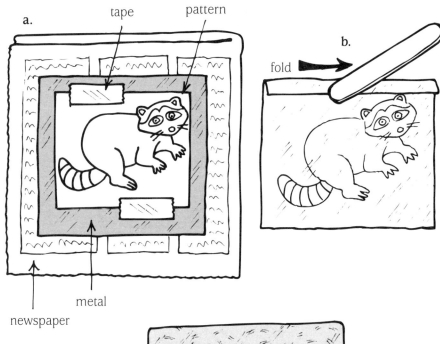

a. tape pattern

b. fold

metal

newspaper

Animal Patterns

Nature Pouch (30-45 minutes)

Materials

- Nature Pouch Pattern (p. 91)
- clear Con-Tact® paper
- twine or leather lacing
- variety of decorative papers (scrapbook paper, magazine pages, nature colored card stock, construction paper, and gift wrap, etc.)
- stickers (a variety of theme-related stickers are available from Gospel Light)
- glass, acrylic or wooden beads with large holes

Standard Supplies

- paper
- scissors
- craft sticks
- masking tape
- hole punches

Preparation

Photocopy Nature Pouch Pattern, making one for each child. Cut Con-Tact paper into 7x9½-inch (18x24-cm) rectangles, preparing two for each child. Cut twine into 5-foot (1.5-m) lengths, preparing one for each child.

Instruct each child in the following procedures:

- Peel the paper backing off of a sheet of Con-Tact paper. Place sticky-side up over Nature Pouch Pattern. You will be able to see the pattern through the Con-Tact paper (sketch a).

Tip: Lick fingers to keep Con-Tact paper from sticking to them as you work.

- Select some decorative papers and tear them into different shapes. Place on Con-Tact paper, decorative side up. (Make sure you cover the area over the pattern.) Decorate with stickers (sketch b).
- Peel the paper backing off the second sheet of Con-Tact paper. Carefully place over the paper collage you created, sticky side down. Rub over surface of Con-Tact paper with the edge of a craft stick (sketch c).
- Make two masking-tape loops. Place each loop on the back of pattern page, behind each pattern piece. Stick pattern to paper collage (sketch d). Cut out pattern pieces. The masking tape loops will hold the pattern pieces onto each pouch piece as it is cut apart.
- Use hole punch to punch holes through pouch pieces as shown on patterns (sketch e).
- Line up the bottoms of the two pattern pieces. Starting at the upper right side of the pouch, lace twine or lacing through the holes in both pattern pieces (sketch f).
- When you've laced all the way around the pouch, slip a lanyard hook onto one end of the twine or lacing and tie a knot. Add a couple beads to each tail end and knot to secure. Fold flap over front of pouch.

Enrichment Ideas

- Punch two holes in the center front of the pouch for a latch bead. As you are lacing around the edges, make a loop in the center of the top. Use a scrap piece of twine or lacing to thread a large bead through the center holes and knot to secure. This will make a latch to secure your pouch.
- Photocopy verses and/or the Daily Truth statement onto pieces of card stock or colored paper. Children cut out and put inside their pouches.

tape loop on back of pattern

Nature Pouch Pattern

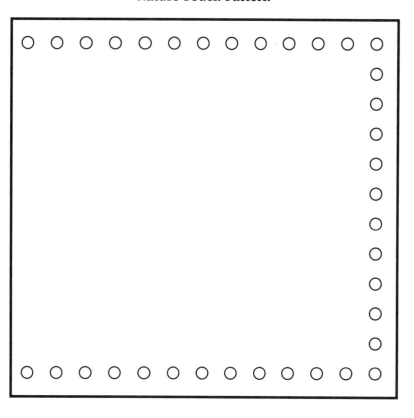

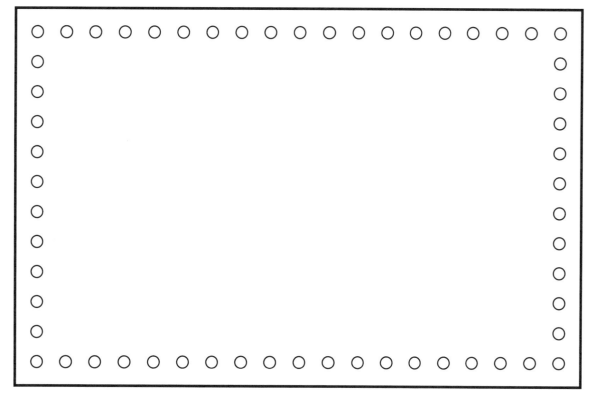

Conversation

Inside our pouches, we can put pictures, copies of the verses or other things we are learning this week at Son-Rock Kids Camp. In 1 John 3:1 our Bibles tell us "How great is the love the Father has lavished on us, that we should be called children of God!" What a great way to remember that we are loved and accepted by Jesus!

• Older Elementary • Grades 4-6 •

Clay Critters (20-30 minutes)

Materials

- 2-oz. (60-ml) packages of polymer clay (provide a variety of colors including brown, tan, black, white and pink or red)

Tip: Custom colors of polymer clay can be made by blending colors together. Choose the colors you want to blend (such as brown and tan for a lighter shade of brown) and work the clay between your hands until the colors are blended together.

- resealable plastic bags, snack or sandwich size
- toothpicks
- baking sheets

For each child—
- plastic knife
- sheet of waxed paper
- ruler

Standard Supplies

- markers
- index cards

Preparation

Open polymer clay packages and use plastic knife to cut each block in half, creating 1-oz. (30-ml) pieces. (Note: The amount of polymer clay you will need depends on the animals children choose to create, and the number of animals they make. Minimally, provide at least 1 oz. for each student.) Place each piece of clay in a separate resealable plastic bag and seal.

Conversation

All of the animals we made belong in a forest or woodland area. It would be weird to find a giraffe in the forest. If we're in a new place or with people we don't know well, we might not feel accepted. All of us face times when we don't feel we belong. But Jesus wants you to know that He loves and accepts you, just the way you are. And if you choose to, you can become a member of **God's family.** (Invite students interested in knowing more about becoming members of God's family to talk with you or another teacher after class. See "Leading a Child to Christ," p. 6.)

Instruct each child in the following procedures:

- Before making any animals, you will need to condition the clay. Remove clay from bag and play with the clay, kneading, folding and rolling it for a couple of minutes. Conditioning the clay makes it easier to work with, and ensures the final result will not easily break. The clay is conditioned when you can roll it into a log, fold it and the clay doesn't break (see sketch).
- Follow instructions for the animal of your choice, or make an animal using your own design.
- After class, leader places baking sheets in oven and bakes according to polymer clay manufacturer's instructions. (Usually 265° F or 275° F for an hour.) You can bake in either a regular oven or toaster oven. Allow animals to cool before removing from baking sheet.

Tip: To simplify this craft for the students. Put the materials needed for each critter in individual bags with a set of instructions for that critter. Make a variety of critter bags.

Enrichment Idea

Students make bugs as well as animals. Provide chenille wires for students to use to make antennae or legs.

To Make Bear—

- Use a 1-oz. (30-ml) piece of clay to form the body. Condition the clay. Roll it in your hands to make an oblong shape. Push one end down on waxed paper sheet. This will be the body of your bear (sketch a).

- Use another 1-oz. (30-ml) piece of clay in the same color. Condition the clay and then roll into a log 4 inches (10 cm) long. Make cuts at 1 1/2 inches (4 cm), 2 inches (5 cm) and 3 inches (7.5 cm) (sketch b). You will have two 1-inch (2.5-cm) pieces, a 1 1/2-inch (4 cm) piece and a 1/2-inch (1.3-cm) piece.

- Use the 1 1/2-inch (4-cm) piece to make the head. Roll into a ball. Break a toothpick in half and stick it in the bear's body. Place head on top of toothpick (sketch c).

- Cut the 1/2-inch piece into four pieces the same size. Roll into pea-sized balls. Flatten balls with finger. Pinch the bottoms of two flattened pieces to make ears and place on top of head, flattening pinched edge to top of head. Place the other two flattened pieces on face to make cheeks (sketch d).

- Take one of the 1-inch (2.5-cm) pieces and cut it in half. Roll one half piece into a ball, and then make a long teardrop shape. Flatten the small end of the tear drop and attach to the side of the bear to make an arm. Repeat with the other half piece (sketch e).

- Take the last 1-inch (2.5-cm) piece and cut it in half. Roll each piece into a short thick log. Flatten one end and stick under bear to make legs (sketch f).

- Add final details to your bear using scraps of white clay. Make circles for eyes and place on head. Put black beads in the centers of eyes for pupils. Add a bead for a nose. Use your toothpick to poke "whiskers" on the bear's cheeks and to make claws on all four paws. Use more white or tan clay scraps to make circles for paws and an oval for the bear's chest.

- Write your name on an index card. Carefully lift bear from waxed-paper sheet and place on index card. Place index card on a baking sheet or other place designated by the craft leader.

a.   b.   c.   d.   e.   f.

To Make Rabbit—

- Condition a 1-oz. (30-ml) piece of clay, and then roll into a log 5 inches (12.5 cm) long. Cut into five 1-inch (2.5-cm) pieces (sketch a).
- Combine two of the pieces to make the rabbit's body. Roll clay in your hands to make an oblong shape. Push one end down on waxed paper sheet (sketch b).
- Use another piece to make the head. Roll into an oblong. Break a toothpick in half and stick it in the rabbit's body. Place head on top of toothpick (sketch c).
- Cut one of the remaining pieces of clay in four pieces. Take one of the pieces and cut it in half. Roll each piece into a ball and then flatten to make an oblong. Place on either side of rabbit's body. Combine the other three pieces together and roll into a log. Flatten log and cut in half to form the two feet.

- Place cut ends under rabbit body and fold feet up over rabbit belly (sketch d).
- Cut last piece of clay in half to form the ears. Roll into a ball, and then roll on one end to form a teardrop shape. Flatten teardrop to make ears. Apply one ear to either side of rabbit's head. Slightly curl the ends up (sketch e).
- Roll scraps of white clay into pea-sized pieces and flatten. Place on face to make cheeks. Form a triangle from a small scrap of pink clay and place above cheeks to make nose. Place two black beads above nose for eyes. Poke cheeks with toothpick to make "whiskers." Also use toothpick to draw eyebrows, mouth, and claws on hands and feet (sketch f).
- Write your name on an index card. Carefully lift rabbit from waxed-paper sheet and place on index card. Place index card on a baking sheet or other place designated by the craft leader.

To Make Skunk—

- Condition a 1-oz. (30-ml) piece of clay, and then roll into a log 3 inches (7.5 cm) long. Cut into a 2-inch (5-cm) piece and a 1-inch (2.5-cm) piece (sketch a).
- Set the 1-inch (2.5-cm) piece aside for the tail and legs. Now take the 2-inch (5-cm) piece, roll it into a log 3 inches (7.5 cm) long and again, cut a 2-inch (5-cm) piece (for the body) and a 1-inch (2.5-cm) piece (for the head).
- Roll the 2-inch piece into an oblong to form the body. Place it on waxed paper sheet.
- Take the small piece and form a gum-drop shape. Slightly pinch the fatter end of the piece and cut in half. Shape each cut section into ears (sketch b).
- Pick up the piece you set aside earlier for the tail and legs. Roll into a log 3 inches (7.5 cm) long and again, cut a 2-inch (5-cm) piece (for the tail) and a 1-inch (2.5-cm) piece (for the legs).
- Form the tail by rolling a ball, and then pressing on one end and rolling to form a teardrop shape. Flatten to form a tail longer and fatter than the skunk's body. Press small end of tail under back of skunk and curl tail up and over (sketch c).
- Form the legs by cutting the remaining piece into four pieces, and rolling them into balls. Flatten one end of each ball and stick under the skunk to form the legs (sketch c).
- Take scrap white clay and form a long thin teardrop shape. Flatten it. Starting between the ears, place stripe over head, body and along tail of skunk. Use knife to trim stripe if needed (sketch d).
- Take more scrap white clay and form two eyes. Put black beads in centers for pupils. Use toothpick to form a mouth and to put claws on the paws (sketch d).
- Write your name on an index card. Carefully lift skunk from waxed-paper sheet and place on index card. Place index card on a baking sheet or other place designated by the craft leader.

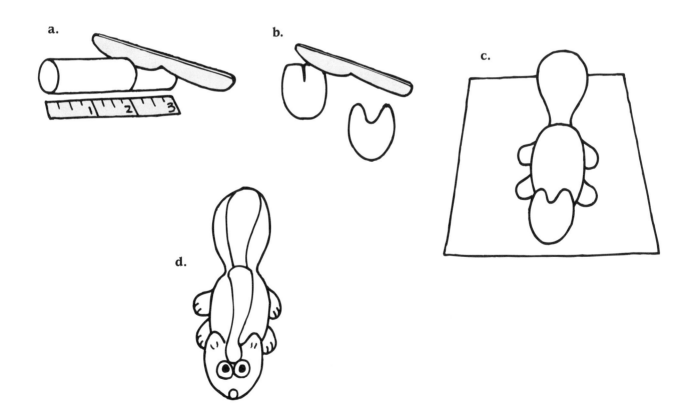

Wire Wraps (20-30 minutes)

Materials

- Wire Wraps Patterns (p. 97)
- 16- or 18-gauge craft wire
- 24- or 26-gauge craft wire
- wire cutters
- variety of beads
- monofilament (clear fishing line)

Standard Supplies

- card stock
- scissors
- measuring stick

Preparation

On card stock, photocopy Wire Wraps Patterns, enlarging so that each pattern is about 5 inches (12.5 cm) in size. Cut to separate patterns (you need not cut out each pattern). Make multiple copies of each pattern and make sure there is at least one pattern for each child.

Use wire cutters to cut 16- or 18-gauge craft wire and 24- or 26-gauge craft wire into 24-inch (61-cm) pieces. Prepare one 16- or 18-gauge piece and two or three 24- or 26-gauge pieces for each child.

Conversation

Some of you chose to make a cross today. The cross reminds us of our Bible story and that Jesus died on a cross. But He didn't stay dead! Jesus died and came alive again to be our Savior and to save us from the consequences of breaking God's rules. In Romans 10:9 our Bible says, "If you confess with your mouth, 'Jesus is Lord,' and believe in your heart that God raised him from the dead, you will be saved." When we are saved by Jesus, we become members of God's family forever!

Instruct each child in the following procedures:

- Select a pattern. Following the pattern, bend 16- or 18-gauge wire around the outline (sketch a).
- When you get back to the beginning, trim wire, making sure both ends overlap about ¹/₂ inch (1.3 cm) (sketch b).
- Using a piece of 24- or 26-gauge wire, tightly wrap around the overlapping wire ends (sketch c).
- Then wrap wire across the design in multiple directions. Continue wrapping wire, occasionally adding beads, until you get to end of wire. Tightly wrap end like you did at the beginning. If you want, you may continue wrapping with one or more pieces of 24- or 26-gauge wire.
- Cut off a piece of monofilament (clear fishing line) about 8-inches (20.5-cm) long. Thread through top of wire shape and tie a knot to make a hanger. Hang shape on a wall, doorknob or drawer pull, or place in a window as a sun-catcher.

Enrichment Ideas

- Instead of paper patterns, provide cookie cutters. Children wrap 16- or 18-gauge wire around cookie cutters to create wire shapes.
- Make smaller shapes and attach to a length of ribbon to make necklaces or bookmarks.

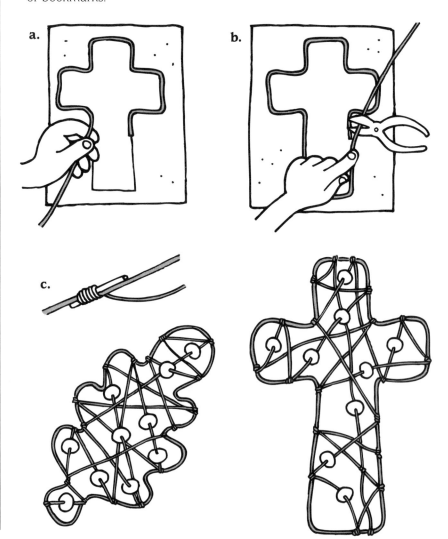

Nature Object Candle Holder (20-30 minutes)

Materials

- nature objects (pebbles, dried beans and seeds, etc.)
- low-temperature glue guns and glue sticks

Optional—
- 3M® Quick Dry Tacky Adhesive or Elmer's® Probond Stix-All

For each child—
- 3-inch (7.5-cm) Styrofoam or floral foam sphere or block
- marker
- plastic knife
- tea-light candle

Conversation

Candles bring light to dark rooms, and even in a well-lit room can help us feel warm and protected. Jesus helps and protects us in every situation. Our candle holders can remind us of Jesus' protection. Discuss with children Bible stories they know where Jesus helped and protected others.

Instruct each child in the following procedures:

- If you are using a sphere, cut a slice from sphere to form the bottom (sketch a).
- Place tea-light candle on top of sphere. Trace around bottom of candle (sketch b).
- Use knife to cut out opening for candle (sketch c). Place candle in opening and press down, to make sure candle stands firmly in base (sketch d).
- Decorate your candle holder using glue gun (or optional adhesives) and nature objects of your choice. If decorating a sphere, start in the middle and glue a line of pebbles, beans or seeds (sketch e).
- Place rows of additional materials above and below the first row until sphere is covered. If decorating a block, start around the candle and work outward from there.

Enrichment Idea

If decorating candle holders with pebbles, after class, leader sprays pebbles with a clear acrylic gloss to make them shine and the colors more intense.

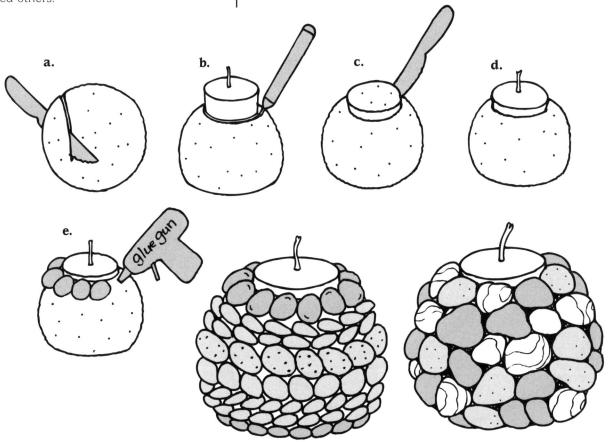

Fresh-Start Rainbows (20-30 minutes)

Materials

- plastic beads in blue, green, yellow and red
- baking sheets
- monofilament (clear fishing line)

For each child—
- 1 each of chenille wires in blue, green, yellow and red
- sheet of waxed paper

Standard Supplies

- permanent markers
- scissors

Conversation

Rainbows appear as the sun starts to shine through falling rain. They can remind us of the fresh start we get through Jesus' forgiveness. Even when we do wrong things, Jesus doesn't give up on us. He loves us. In Psalm 86:5 our Bible says, "You are forgiving and good, O Lord, abounding in love to all who call to you." All we have to do is ask, and Jesus will forgive us.

Instruct each child in the following procedures:

- String a blue bead onto blue chenille wire. Bend wire up to hold bead in place (sketch a).
- Continue stringing beads until chenille wire is almost full. Bend end of wire up over last bead. Bend wire into an upside-down U and place on waxed paper (sketch b).
- String green beads onto green chenille wire as before. When wire is almost full, bend wire into a U shape and place inside blue wire. Add or remove beads as necessary so that green wire fits inside blue wire (sketch c).
- Insert the bent ends of green wires into the blue beads (sketch d).
- Repeat process for yellow and red chenille wires.
- When rainbow is complete, use permanent marker to write name on sheet of waxed paper. Place rainbow on waxed paper sheet on baking sheet.
- After class, leader makes sure beads are touching on each rainbow and then places baking sheets in toaster oven placed outside or other oven in well-ventilated area and bakes at 350° F for ten minutes. It is important that the baking occurs in a well-ventilated area as the plastic beads are fusing together. There will be an unpleasant odor. Allow rainbows to cool before removing from baking sheet. Add loops of monofilament (clear fishing line) to make hangers for rainbows.

Simplification Idea

Students make designs with varying sizes of beads on chenille wires and add clear fishing line without baking.

Enrichment Idea

Provide copies of Wire Wrap Patterns. Instead of making rainbows, students make other designs of their own choice. Provide scrap paper for children to sketch their designs.

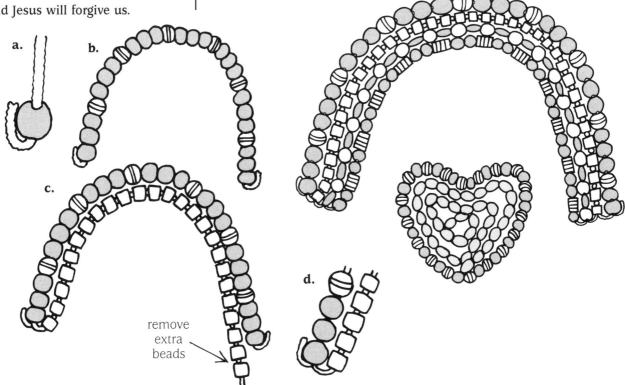

a. b.

c.

remove extra beads

d.

Natural Frame (30-45 minutes)

Materials

- cardboard
- dried or silk leaves
- low-temperature glue guns and glue sticks
- thin sticks or twigs
- twine
- natural decorations (dried or silk flowers, pebbles, etc.)

Standard Supplies

- scissors
- masking tape
- hole punch

Preparation

Cut cardboard into 7x9-inch (18x23-cm) pieces, one for each student. In the center of each piece of cardboard, measure and draw a 4x6-inch (10x15-cm) opening (sketch a).

Conversation

In your frame, you can put a picture of yourself here at SonRock Kids Camp. What are some of your favorite things you have done this week? The Bible tells us about a man whose legs didn't work. He wasn't able to run and play games like we do. He could only beg for money. But when Peter chose to help the man, Jesus' power made the man well. After that, the man could walk and run and jump! Peter showed he was living for Jesus when he helped the man. Every day, we can live for Jesus, too, by doing the good things Jesus has planned for us to do!

Instruct each child in the following procedures:

- Use glue gun to glue leaves to frame, overlapping leaves as you go (sketch b).
- Use hole punch to punch a hole in each corner of the frame (sketch c).
- Arrange sticks and twigs around perimeter of frame, trimming as needed. Wrap sticks at each corner with twine, and run twine through hole in frame to attach frame to sticks (sketch d). Secure twine in a knot and trim. Dot knot with glue to secure. Make a loose loop around sticks at top of frame and tie to form a hanging loop.
- Decorate by gluing pebbles and dried or silk flowers to frame (sketch e).

Enrichment Idea

Print a memory verse on a piece of decorative paper and glue to the front of the frame.

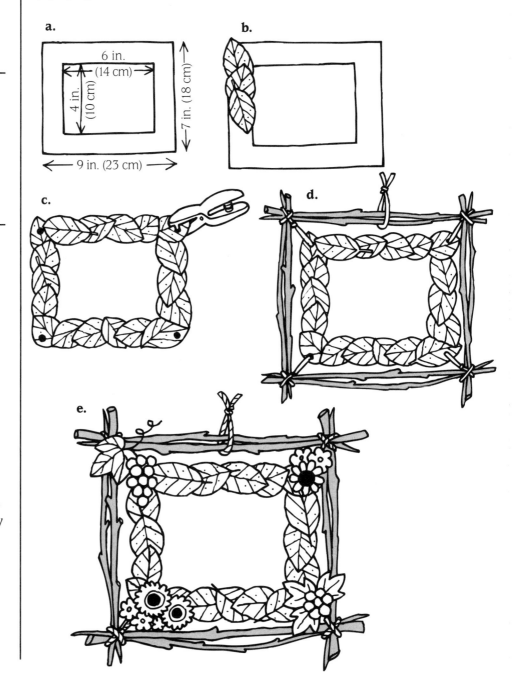

Twig Weaving (20-30 minutes)

Materials

- small forked twigs or branches
- variety of stringing material (yarn, raffia, twine, etc.)
- pruning shears
- nature objects (feathers, pods, leaves, etc.)

For each child—
- mason jar

Standard Supplies

- scissors

Conversation

Our Twig Weavings allow us to place different objects in a place where we can see them every day. Seeing them will remind us of what we've learned here at Son-Rock Kids Camp. Every day, we've heard true stories from the Bible. We've heard that Peter needed Jesus' forgiveness. Jesus forgave Peter and gave him a fresh start! We can receive Jesus' forgiveness, too. All we have to do is ask for it.

Instruct each child in the following procedures:

- Select two or more forked twigs or branches and wrap stringing material around the base of the twigs or branches (sketch a). Use pruning shears to trim off extra branches or twigs.
- Tie end of yarn or other stringing material to the bottom of one branch. Weave yarn over and under the other branches, working from one side to the other. Then weave back the other way (sketch b). Continue weaving until you are pleased with the results.
- Weave feathers, pods, leaves and other nature objects into the woven design. Write a memory verse on a scrap of paper and place in branches or in between weaving.
- Wrap raffia or other stringing material around the neck of a mason jar. Place Twig Weaving in jar and fill with pebbles.

Budget Tip: Look for potpourri made from large nature objects. A large bag with a variety of objects can be found for only a few dollars at most craft stores.

Alternate Idea

Do weaving outdoors, between two or more trees. Children weave back and forth between trees, and then place nature objects, pictures, photos, verse papers, etc. in the weavings.

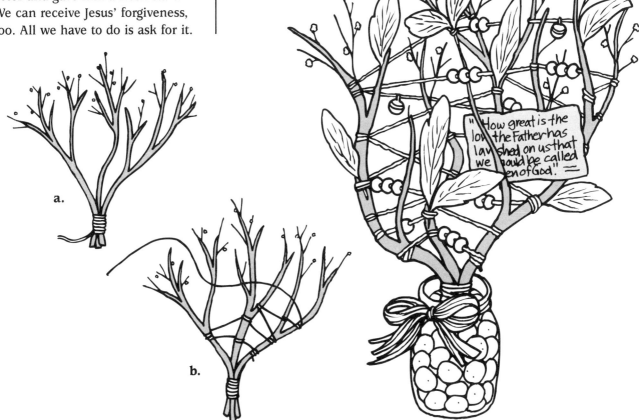

a.

b.

"How great is the love the Father has lavished on us that we would be called en of God!" —

• Older Elementary • Grades 4-6 •   **101**

Nature Words (10-25 minutes)

Materials

- nature materials (sticks, twigs, feathers, wire-stemmed silk or plastic flowers, etc.)
- chenille wires
- pruning shears
- stringing material (yarn, leather lacing, etc.)

For each child—

- sturdy stick or branch 18 to 24 inches (45.5 to 61 cm) long

Standard Supplies

- scissors
- craft glue

Conversation

We've talked about these words a lot at SonRock Kids Camp. They each have a very special meaning. Darryl, why did you make the word "Saved"? Why is that word important to you? In Romans 10:9 our Bible says, "If you confess with your mouth, 'Jesus is Lord,' and believe in your heart that God raised him from the dead, you will be saved."

Instruct each child in the following procedures:

- Use chenille wires or nature materials to form the letters of one of the key words from each session: "Accepted," "Protected," "Saved," "Forgiven" or "Living" (sketch a). Use pruning shears or scissors to trim as needed.
- Glue letters or attach with chenille wires to sturdy stick or branch.
- Tie a length of stringing material to each end of the word stick to form a hanger. You may wish to string additional nature materials on the stringing material.

a.

Index of Crafts

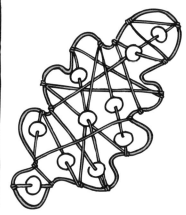

"If you confess with your mouth, 'Jesus is Lord,' and believe in your heart that God raised him from the dead, you will be saved." Romans 10:9